ROOTS FOR A NEW RHETORIC

Roots for
A New Rhetoric

DANIEL FOGARTY, S.J.

DEAN, THE SCHOOL OF EDUCATION
SAINT MARY'S UNIVERSITY, HALIFAX, CANADA

NEW YORK / RUSSELL & RUSSELL

Foreword

WITH HIS CHARACTERISTIC CONCERN FOR RESPONSIBLE AND perspicuous statement, James Reston writes in this morning's *New York Times:*

> President Eisenhower has finally cut through the tedious rhetoric and propaganda of the foreign ministers' conference in Geneva and stated his guiding principles for negotiating with Premier Nikita S. Krushchev on the future of Germany. . . .

With Father Daniel Fogarty's *Roots for a New Rhetoric* also before me, "tedious rhetoric" seems almost to be set in boldface type. And the pertinence of his study to the education of the new generation who will handle negotiations for the future of world culture comes clear. For Father Fogarty is first of all a teacher, concerned with new scholarship and teaching methods that will help college freshmen to master the spirit and forms of oral and written expression appropriate to the modes of communication of contemporary culture.

Father Fogarty has a thorough understanding of modern studies in communication—psychological, sociological, literary, historical—that are leading many thoughtful people to see that the fundamental changes in patterns of communication are both index and agent to corresponding changes in our culture. He is also a classical scholar, with easy access to the rhetorics of Greece and Rome and their synthesis in the teaching patterns of the Scholastic trivium. From these scholarly backgrounds he reexamines the term "rhetoric," both as an aspect of a philosophy of communication and as an area of instruction in freshman courses variously labelled Rhetoric I, English I, Composition, Communication Skills, and so on. His concern is not to propose a new synthesis for the twentieth century. He seeks, rather, to describe briefly the characteristics of earlier rhetorics—of Aristotle, Cicero, Quintilian, Ramus, for instance, as responses to communication needs of their day—and then to describe in detail currently emerging conceptions of rhetoric, recognizing them as the responses of individual scholars to their perceptions of communication needs today. He provides useful supplements and alternatives to classical rhetoric, which are adaptable to instruction *about* communication as a human phenomenon and to instruction *in* the uses of language, whether alone or in mutually reenforcing combination with other symbols in motion picture, television, radio, or four-color press.

Principal spokesmen for the "new rhetoric" in the present volume are I. A. Richards, Kenneth Burke, and S. I. Hayakawa, who, through sustained correspondence and conference with Father Fogarty, lend authority and immediacy to his delineation of their philosophies of rhetoric. Richards' sources lie deep in Plato, Aristotle, Coleridge, and George Campbell, whose "art of adapting discourse to its end" he borrows as his own definition of rhetoric. With his interest in relatively recent studies in information theory, and from his earlier psycho–biological–anthropological orientation, Richards provides the roots of a rhetoric significant to reader and listener as well as to writer and speaker. He directs attention to the conscious process by which authors and audiences arrive at mutual understanding. Kenneth Burke acknowledges background in Aristotle and Bergson and Remy de Gourmont. This philosophic base, plus his modern socio-psychological orientation, provides the roots for a rhetoric which includes all human action as symbolic gesture. He turns primary attention to ways in which we communicate with ourselves and with others to arrive at the "residual compromise" essential to the resolution of personal and interpersonal frictions and disharmonies. In S. I. Hayakawa (and his mathematically–psychiatrically oriented associates from Korzybski to Rapaport, Lee, and Johnson) Father Fogarty finds roots for a rhetoric that seeks attitudes and processes for maintaining personal balance and for arriving at decisions in the conference–committee context which characterizes legislative, political, industrial, and community action today.

The philosophies of rhetoric of Richards, Burke, and the General Semanticists are all a far cry from the pejorative "tedious rhetoric." Their comparative presentation is informative for teachers of the freshman course, who, if we judge aright from programs of the Conference on College Composition and Communication over the past ten years, are seeking a scholarly rationale broad enough to embrace oral and written composition, approaches to literary criticism, media studies, and descriptive linguistics. Some teachers find this rationale in the term communication itself; others will find reassurance in Father Fogarty's exposition of the disciplines of a new rhetoric, redefined in the context of modern studies in communication.

Beyond careful delineation of newer ideas of rhetoric, Father Fogarty's study provides a number of starting points for productive speculation on the nature of language and the importance of instruction *in* and *about* language. He works from the perspective, for instance, that in any period of culture change, language, carrying the content of the culture—its facts, ideas, values, and relationships—is the key point for investigation of and participation in directing that change. Again, he invites his readers to play with varied senses of the term "language arts": (1) as the term used in elementary and secondary schools to designate instruction in the skills of reading, writing, speaking, and listening; (2) as the historic term for the arts of language—rhetoric, logic, grammar; (3) as the correlates of other arts, whose changing forms and processes students also observe as symbols of culture in their broad courses in the humanities; (4) as the simultaneously active rhetoric–logic–grammar involved in every communicative act, a unity sometimes lost sight of on campuses where instruction in rhetoric is left to departments of speech, instruction in logic goes forward in departments of philosophy and mathematics, and instruction in grammar remains isolated in departments of English.

The scope of Father Fogarty's study is obviously broad, though it maintains focus on what we might call the survival values of sound instruction in a modern rhetoric of "peace and union," to use Burke's term. In breadth and focus it joins with related studies undertaken in our coordinating seminars for research in the teaching of languages and linguistics, humanities and communication. Ken Macrorie's *Objectivity and Responsibility in Newspaper Reporting* examines these key terms in process of redefinition, with an eye to bringing instruction in communication courses into line with practice in modern journalism. William T. Beauchamp's *Peirce's Conception of the Symbolic Process*, completed just before his death early this year, dwells revealingly on George Campbell's *The Philosophy of Rhetoric*, which was Peirce's textbook at Harvard. These and comparable studies now in progress, dealing with emerging conceptions of logic and with other aspects of the symbolic process, should provide scholarly base for progressive improvement of instruction in communication arts, skill, and media—and a gradual redefinition of rhetoric that links it inseparably with the other arts of language and these with other arts in our culture.

FRANCIS SHOEMAKER

Teachers College
Columbia University
June 4, 1959

Contents

ROOTS FOR A NEW RHETORIC

Introduction

LANGUAGE IS MAN'S MOST SIGNIFICANT INVENTION. IT CONTAINS the accumulated experience of his race—its facts, ideas, feelings, values, and relationships. It makes possible the most important range of his specifically human activity and allows him to project the imaginative ideals that make such activity worth while. It is through language that we have Hellenic literature, preventive medicine, and the Bill of Rights. Out of language symbols, man has fashioned the exquisite sensitivity of Hamlet, the instruments of psychotherapy, and that sizable but sensible dream that became the United Nations. Clearly, for whatever man creates or improves, conserves or communicates, language is of central importance.

This importance of language seems to be most deeply realized at times of major crisis and change. Educators, businessmen, and diplomats are acutely conscious of it in the present era of crisis. Francis Shoemaker, writing from the University of Wisconsin in 1949, emphasized this consciousness among educators.[1]

[1] Francis Shoemaker, "Self-Realization, Communication, and Aesthetic Experience," in *Communication in General Education*, ed. Earl J. McGrath (Dubuque, Iowa: William C. Brown Company, 1949), pp. 234–235.

In the introductory pamphlet of a series on communication published by the National Council of Teachers of English, Lennox Grey had already indicated the broad range of this same consciousness:

Communication means not only the instruments and physical lines of communication that must link our men and machines all over the world but embraces all those media and processes—social, psychological, artistic, linguistic—which are at work in the exchange of information, ideas and common feelings on which the health and moral stamina of any community depend.[2]

The interest of businessmen in language is readily apparent in the advertising and entertainment industries. The development of simultaneous translation for use in the general sessions of the United Nations is evidence that diplomats are also aware of the central importance of language.

There are at least two reasons for the present-day realization that language is at the center of most of our thinking. To begin with, the past quarter-century has been the coming-of-age period for a whole family of newer sciences, such as sociology, anthropology, psychiatry, and the newer applications of psychology. The connection between these new sciences and the renewed interest in language is much more than coincidental. Psychologists tell us that verbal communication has much to do with mental health. Sociologists and anthropologists, searching for solutions to our own problems in the patterns of other cultures, have discovered that words can build hatred and that a people's language can tell much of their story. Psychiatrists have found that it is in the mental patient's verbal expression of his trouble that science must look for healing and remedy. And scientists began to realize again, in this age as in the past, that the very tabulation of their measured conclusions was helplessly dependent upon language. Su-

[2] Lennox Grey, *What Communication Means Today*, NCTE Pamphlets on Communication (Chicago: National Council of Teachers of English, 1944), p. 29.

sanne Langer, speaking of symbolism, clearly includes language when she says:

Quotations could be multiplied almost indefinitely, from an imposing list of sources—from John Dewey and Bertrand Russell, from Brunschwicg and Piaget and Head, Kohler and Koffka, Carnap, Delacroix, Ribot, Cassirer, Whitehead—from philosophers, psychologists, neurologists, and anthropologists—to substantiate the claim that symbolism is the recognized key to that mental life which is characteristically human and above the level of sheer animality.[3]

The other reason for this increased emphasis on language might well be its easily observable power of communication as used in the public arts. No one who has witnessed the nationwide appeal for food rationing during World War II, or the dividends that advertising pays to the manufacturer of a "status" motor car, or the meteoric rise to popularity of a television comedian, needs to be told that language, through the public arts, has become as promisingly powerful, and as dangerously so, as any other force in modern life.

Rhetoric, as the pedagogical instrument for learning the increasingly important uses of language, has shared in the general recognition of the importance of language. If language needs reexamination and study, then rhetoric, whether written or spoken, needs reexamination too. The same critical conditions that focus attention on language, that make us reexamine its roots and adapt it to our needs, call for the same reexamination and adaptation of rhetoric, the art by which we not only use language but also learn its uses.

Three theories of rhetoric have emerged during the past quarter-century in response to this new emphasis upon and reexamination of language and the language arts. The three theories are to be found in the works of I. A. Richards, of Kenneth Burke, and of the General Semanticists who are represented by Alfred

[3] Susanne K. Langer, *Philosophy in a New Key* (Cambridge, Mass.: Harvard University Press, 1951), pp. 27–28.

3

Korzybski, S. I. Hayakawa, Irving J. Lee, and others. In this volume these three theories will be examined carefully.

It is hoped that this inquiry into the three theories will provide educators and formulators of general education courses with most of the elements, old and new, that promise to make rhetoric a better classroom instrument.

The term "rhetoric," as it is used in this study, stands for the art of prose expression, written or oral. In classical times rhetoric was understood to mean the persuasion of many by one speaker. Later it came to include written persuasion and even exposition. In our own times it signifies persuasion in many forms, in language, in visual symbols, and in symbols of status. Most important of all, perhaps, it has come to mean the ways of arriving at mutual understanding among people working toward patterns of cooperative action. Beyond this, the intimate relationships between rhetoric and the other language arts of grammar and logic are again beginning to be recognized. The term "philosophy of rhetoric" includes the epistemological, logical, and psychological questions which lie at the base of the art of rhetoric. It puts special emphasis upon those problems which the three theories contend are most pertinent to rhetoric—word–thought–thing relationships, definition, abstraction, theory of metaphor, and theory of style. The ancient term "teaching rhetoric" refers to the courses and manuals that teach the art of expression.

Chapter 1 of this volume provides the setting for the study of the three theories of rhetoric. It contains a historical sketch of rhetoric from Corax of Syracuse, in about 460 B.C., up to the nineteen-twenties, and analyzes the current traditional theory.

Chapters 2, 3, and 4 present in detail each of the three theories of rhetoric. I. A. Richards, from a linguistic background that pointed up the problems of meaning, offers a nearly complete philosophy of rhetoric that culminates in his seven instruments of interpretation. Kenneth Burke makes social and psychoanalytic extensions of the Aristotelian philosophy of rhetoric with his theory of verbalized motivation. The General Semanticists, represented principally by S. I. Hayakawa and Irving J. Lee, and working from the Korzybskian principle that sanity today hinges upon a revision of yesterday's outmoded Aristotelian terminology, offer what amounts to a philosophy of rhetoric in their "non-Aristotelian" system.

Finally, in Chapter 5 an attempt is made to synthesize all the elements in the three philosophies of rhetoric that can be applied to teaching rhetoric. It is an attempt to provide, for teachers and formulators of courses, a survey of the promising elements of current theory in rhetoric so that they may make the choices and adaptations that suit the needs of their first-year courses, variously titled English I, composition, the writing of speeches, and communication. Clearly such a synthesis will have to answer the social and educational challenges of the approaching decade.

The emergence today of three philosophies of rhetoric seems to have historical significance. In Aristotle's time philosophy itself was taught each day along with rhetoric, and in such close coordination that there could have been no call for any explicit philosophy of rhetoric. The peripatetic principles of a very complete logic and of a rudimentary epistemology and psychology were fresh in Athenian students' minds as they studied and practiced the elements of what we now call Aristotle's "Rhetorica." And through all the centuries since then, rhetoric has almost always had its roots in the general philosophy of Aristotle. The apparent revolt of the Sophists, and of Bacon and Ramus and Campbell, affected the teaching of rhetoric much more than its philosophy. And when general philosophy itself changed radically with Descartes and with the later German and English philosophers from the sixteenth to the nineteenth centuries, rhetoric was still relatively undisturbed by the changes. It met the crises in its long history with shifts of emphasis—now upon style, now upon its aim and content—without changing or even taking any special notice of its basic philosophy which was still

5

presumably Aristotelian. The point is not so much that rhetoric did not change its philosophy with the changing philosophic times, but that for twenty-three hundred years little or no interest was shown in any kind of philosophy of rhetoric.

And while, during the whole span of these centuries, there was no real philosophy of rhetoric, there were some demands for it. Cicero pointed to its importance in his day. The medieval Scholastics took the Thomistic interpretation of Aristotelian general philosophy along with the rhetoric of the trivium and had no need to call for a specific philosophy of rhetoric. Bacon skirted the edges of this need for the deeper consideration of the philosophical basis of a language communication. Archbishop Whately recognized its importance but, unfortunately, did not do very much about it. Campbell probably came closest to a philosophy of rhetoric. He treated ambiguity and interpretation, but with scarcely enough fullness or direction to amount to a complete theory of definition. Since Aristotle, then, a few have recognized the need for a philosophy of rhetoric; some even have tried to establish one. But it was really received no sizable amount of attention.

The historically significant point is that within the past thirty-five years three fairly complete philosophies of rhetoric have emerged. These theories not only advocate a revival of the philosophic concerns of rhetoric, but propose the inclusion of such philosophic elements in the actual curricular material of rhetoric itself.

This sudden reappearance of a philosophy of rhetoric, while significant, can scarcely be considered surprising. Rhetoric apparently has come to its present importance through the newly recognized importance of language in general. It might also have been expected to take its philosophic trend from a similar trend in language studies. Certainly many of the outstanding philosophers of our day—thinkers like Peirce, Dewey, Whitehead, Russell, and Black—have been more language-conscious than philosophers of earlier eras. And the sciences, seeking to solve their problems by solving language problems first, have often gone so deeply into language that they can, at least from one point of view, be called philosophies of language. So it seems to be with logicians like Cassirer and Carnap, with linguististic scholars like Ayer and Morris, and with anthropologists like Mannheim, Malinowski, and Sapir. May it not, then, be considered quite the natural result of the philosophical trend in language studies, that rhetoric should begin, even after so long a time, to turn toward philosophy?

Fortunately for the objectivity of this study and for greater depth and richness in its interpretation of the three theories, it has been possible to discuss the first two freely and directly with the men who proposed them. Professor Richards gave full and positive answers to many questions concerning his philosophy of rhetoric and its background which contributed greatly to a better understanding of his books. Frequent and very lengthy conversations with Mr. Burke, as well as numerous and detailed letters and notes, provided insights into his method and theory that might not otherwise have been available. While this was not true of the third theory, the cause of Alfred Korzybski and Irving J. Lee, now deceased, as well as that of Wendell Johnson, was ably represented in personal interview and in letters by Samuel I. Hayakawa. Moreover, each section was carefully read and critically annotated by the sponsor of each theory.

The Background of Rhetoric

IT IS IMPORTANT HERE TO ILLUSTRATE WHAT HAS HAPPENED TO the theory of rhetoric from the earliest times to the present day. This brief sketch is intended as a background for and an introduction to the three current theories of rhetoric that are our main concern. No attempt at definitive history is made. Other students of classical and modern rhetoric have provided ample and reliable material that has been ably summarized in works like those of Thonssen and Baird and of Howell.[1] The intention here is to present the story of rhetoric as it applies to the special purposes of this discussion.

It will help to start by being more definite about what is meant by rhetoric. We are not dealing with oratory or speechmaking, but with the theory of oratory. Our concern will not be with Demosthenes and Pitt and Churchill, but with Aristotle and Ramus and Wilson. More specifically, and with an eye to the

[1] Lester Thonssen and A. Craig Baird, *Speech Criticism* (New York: The Ronald Press Company, 1948) and Wilbur S. Howell, *Logic and Rhetoric in England, 1500–1700* (Princeton, N.J.: Princeton University Press, 1956).

fact that we will be introducing three new philosophies of rhetoric, this historical sketch will emphasize the philosophical theory of rhetoric. And here, philosophical theory simply means those elements of epistemology and psychology that underlie and are presupposed in the general uses of prose communication.

To fulfil its function, then, the chapter is divided into two sections: the chronological events in the history of rhetorical theory with an analysis of that theory as it has developed up to the present day, and the advent of the three new theories discussed in the remainder of the book.

THE STORY OF RHETORIC

Even before the first written *technē* (craft of speech writing) appeared among the Greeks, there were clear evidences of some rhetorical forms. In the *Iliad* and the *Odyssey* of Homer, characters like Achilles and Nestor made speeches and addresses to court favor, to exhort soldiers in battle, or to prove a point. These speeches clearly show some consciousness of organization and invention for the purpose of persuasion.[2] Pericles, too, in the speech paraphrased by Thucydides and known as "The Funeral Oration," appears well versed in the art of epideictic oratory.[3]

But the first known *technē* or textbook came from Sicily. In the year 466 B.C. the citizens of Syracuse revolted against their tyrannical rulers and set up a democracy. A few years later Agrigentum followed suit. The new administrations of these infant democracies, offering justice to all alike, were at first flooded with appeals. Hundreds of citizens filed claims for the redistribution of property seized from them by the tyrants. So many legal cases had to be settled that there was an urgent demand for some method of training in the writing and delivering of appeal and

[2] Thonssen and Baird, *op. cit.*, pp. 29–30.
[3] Thucydides, *The Complete Writings of Thucydides*, trans. P. Crawley (New York: Random House, Inc., 1951), pp. 102–109.

defense speeches in the courts. As often happens, conscious theory seemed to follow unconscious art. Corax of Syracuse, one of the many who must have seen this social need, worked out a theoretical way to prepare speeches in what was the first *technē*, or art of rhetoric.[4] Lester Thonssen and A. Craig Baird point out the three contributions made by Corax to the theory of rhetoric: (1) He considered rhetoric the art of oral persuasion. (2) He divided the speech into five parts: proem, narration, argument, subsidiary remarks, and peroration. (3) He based much of his argumentation on probability, and showed how useful this really was. Tisias, a colleague and successor to Corax at Syracuse, developed the probability element in argumentation even further.[5]

In 427 B.C. a Sophist, Gorgias by name, came to Athens from Leontini, near Syracuse on the same coast of Sicily, and brought with him a speech-making ability he may easily have learned from Corax or Tisias, although his style was different.[6] While he had the cleverness of argumentation that was characteristic of Sicilian oratory, he made much more of beauty of style. This probably suited the aristocratic Athenians very well. Their need for the practical aspects of forensic and political oratory had not reached a peak, and they were able and willing to pay Gorgias well for performing and for teaching their sons to entertain with florid oratory. They listened with delight to his artful and eloquent manipulation of words. That all the citizens did not find plain sense in such eloquence is clear from Plato's "Gorgias," where the Sophist's arguments are criticized as illogical and vain.[7] This florid and artificial style, taught by Protagoras and Isocrates as well,[8] is the element that sharply distinguished the Sophists from the stricter, more plain-spoken Atticists like Corax

[4] J. P. Mahaffy, *A History of Classical Greek Literature* (2nd ed. rev.; London: Longmans, Green, and Co., Ltd., 1883), I, pp. 73–74.
[5] Thonssen and Baird, *op. cit.*, p. 35.   [6] *Ibid.*, pp. 37–38.
[7] Plato, "Gorgias," in *The Dialogues of Plato*, trans. B. Jowett (3rd ed. rev.; New York: Random House, Inc., 1937), I, p. 521.
[8] Thonssen and Baird, *op. cit.*, p. 37.

and Tisias. These two main stems of rhetorical style, the Sophistic floridity and the Atticist simplicity, were to reappear throughout the history of classical oratory.

It was as a zealous antagonist of the dishonesty of sophistic oratory that Plato appears in the history of rhetoric in this same period. His idealistic ethical and educational philosophy in "The Laws" and "The Republic"[9] called for the dialectical method. It was in dialectical discussion that the wise were to communicate wisdom to those not yet wise.[10] But rhetoric, as practiced by both Sophists and Atticists, concerned itself with matters of opinion, with alternatives, neither of which were necessarily true or untrue.[11] Plato had little patience with opinion when there was so much truth to be learned. But as Werner Jaeger remarks, he adequately proves to us that even in matters of opinion it is better to listen to the wise in dialectical form.[12] The "Phaedrus" is itself an example of such teaching in dialectical form.

Plato's most important contribution to rhetoric theory, however, is his insistence upon philosophy and general learning as necessary equipment for the orator or writer. Jaeger makes this evident in his chapter on "Philosophy and Rhetoric" in *Paideia*.[13] It is also insisted upon in the three general admonitions Plato provides in the "Phaedrus": (1) define your terms in the beginning of the speech; (2) acquire wisdom, logic, philosophy, and knowledge of human nature; and (3) divide your material in an orderly manner.[14]

It is important to notice at this point that it seems to have been Plato who put the philosophy into rhetoric. His specific

[9] Plato, *op. cit.*

[10] Werner Jaeger, *Paideia: The Ideals of Greek Culture*, trans. Gilbert Highet (New York: Oxford University Press, 1943), II, pp. 52–57, 62–70, and 309–312.

[11] Plato, "Phaedrus," in *The Dialogues of Plato*, I, pp. 276–282.

[12] Jaeger, *op. cit.*, III (1944), pp. 193–194.

[13] *Ibid.*, III, pp. 182–196.

[14] Plato, *op. cit.*, I, pp. 263–267, 265, and 267–270.

way of introducing it and making it an integral part of rhetorical training was through the method of dialectics. But the main point is that philosophy must go with rhetoric. As Jaeger says: "Whenever any classical school of philosophy paid any attention to rhetoric at all, it always revived this programme."[15]

In the same great century, between 400 and 300 B.C., appeared the greatest rhetorician of them all. Aristotle, as the first great Platonist and as student and fellow teacher with Plato, developed many of his ideas and gave more substance to his dream of a noble rhetoric. Jaeger, still speaking of the importance of philosophy in rhetoric, sums up the transition that took place in the theory of rhetoric from Plato to Aristotle:

He [Plato] could with justice point out that precision and clarity in logical and psychological distinctions are the preconditions of all rhetorical art. He could easily show that, unless he cultivated these intellectual faculties, no orator or writer would be able to convince his audience and his readers; and that the technical tricks taught (then and now) through handbooks of public speaking were no substitute for this type of intellectual training. Plato wrote *Phaedrus* to illuminate this aspect of his paideia and to justify its claim to represent this tendency. It is extremely probable that it was this manifesto which prompted young Aristotle (Plato's pupil, and then a new teacher on the Academy's staff) to bring in rhetoric as a fresh subject in the Platonic curriculum. No doubt he meant to show what a *new* rhetoric could be, if built on the philosophical foundation laid down in the *Phaedrus*.[16]

Most students of Aristotle would admit that he made the greatest contribution to rhetoric up to our time.[17] The "Rhetorica" not only sums up the best of all the elements developed prior to his time but, together with his own and Plato's ideas, forms the best synthesis of any before or since. Beyond this actual manual of rhetoric Aristotle brought to the study of prose expression a whole system of realist philosophy geared to explain everything that was known to man in his time and to organize it with in-

[15] Jaeger, *op. cit.*, III, p. 191.   [16] *Ibid.*, III, pp. 185–186.
[17] Thonssen and Baird, *op. cit.*, pp. 71 and 76.

ternal consistency and logic. Rhetoric, Poetics, Ethics, and Politics were the four pinnacles on the edifice of his system of human knowledge. They were the arts or sets of principles for the arts by which man was to express the great burden of his knowledge.[18]

This foundational philosophy provided rhetoric with explanations for four specific problems that underlie prose expression itself. It is the discussion of these questions which may most properly be called the philosophy of rhetoric, or more loosely, the theory of rhetoric, or the presuppositions of rhetoric. The four problems are: word–thought–thing relationships,[19] abstraction,[20] definition,[21] and argumentation.[22] Aristotle's treatment of these elements is not only the first efficient organization of these ideas but, by and large, is the treatment that has lasted until our day as the philosophy of rhetoric.[23] And since this philosophy of

[18] Aristotle first laid the methodological and epistemological foundations of his system in works like the "Categoriae," "De Interpretatione," "Analytica Priora," and "Analytica Posteriora," and then made causal analyses of everything physical and metaphysical known to man in works like the "Physica," "Metaphysica," "De Anima," and "De Generatione Animalium." As spires to this edifice he formed the separate bodies of principles that might guide the *activities* of men who had all this knowledge in works like the "Politica," "Ethica Nichomachea," "Rhetorica," and "De Poetica." Thus man not only created and knew true, noble, and wise things, but also communicated them to others to promote true, noble, and wise ideas and action. See "Rhetorica" in *The Basic Works of Aristotle*, ed. Richard McKeon, trans. Rhys Roberts *et al.* (New York: Random House, Inc., 1941), i, 5–7 (1362a–1365b). [The Berlin numbers will be appended, in parentheses, to further references to Aristotle's works. They will direct the reader to the correct paragraph in the original edition, first published by Oxford University Press in 1928.]

[19] This is what is sometimes known as "theory of knowing," "epistemology," or "major logic."

[20] For students of Aristotle abstraction would include parts of both the logic and the general metaphysics.

[21] Definition theory analyzes the way in which truth may be attributed to propositions and of course involves both logic and metaphysics.

[22] Argumentation carries the truth of propositions forward to truth in combinations of propositions and involves logic.

[23] That such is the case is evident from a reading of the history of rhetoric, and it will be clearer toward the end of this historical sketch.

rhetoric has lasted and become the traditional explanation of the presuppositions of rhetoric it will be described in more detail in the second part of this chapter.

The "Rhetorica" itself may be summarized briefly as a manual for training the orator, analyzing the emotional and intellectual receptivity of the audience, and writing the speech. The three short books are developed thus: First, the orator must be a man of character, ethically above reproach, and have the emotional, imaginative, and reasoning powers to fit him for his task. He must be armed with the general and specific knowledge he needs for deliberative, epideictic, or forensic oratory, as may suit his purpose. He should understand human nature, the possibilities and probabilities of human reactions to all kinds of things, words, and situations. He should be able to analyze the attitudes of a given audience for a given speech. Then, from a great wealth of *topoi* (sources), he could begin the actual composing. He could pick and choose, accept and reject logical arguments, emotional appeals, figures of speech, appropriate expressions, examples, and so forth, until he had the strongest and most graceful combination of persuasive elements in this one set of circumstances. The next step would be to organize the whole speech so as to give it grace, subtlety, clarity, precision, cogency, power, and interest. Then it would be polished for beauty and clearness of expression in smaller details. Finally, the introduction could be written (or polished, if it had already been written) in such a way that it would win the audience to the orator and to his subject.[24]

Aristotle's definition of rhetoric easily follows from all this. He calls it "the faculty of observing in any given case the available means of persuasion."[25]

In the latter half of the fourth century B.C., when Aristotle

[24] "Rhetorica" in *The Basic Works of Aristotle*, pp. 1325–1451 (1354a–1420b).

[25] *Ibid.*, i, 2, p. 1329 (1355b).

14

already moved down from Macedonia and unified the Greek city—
was writing the "Rhetorica," his illustrious pupil, Alexander, had
states into an alliance under his own standard. He was moving
across Asia and opening passageways for the flow of Hellenic
culture as far as the borders of India. And although Greece had
long since colonized Sicily and the south of Italy with disaffected
citizens, it was not until much later, when the Romans came to
subdue Corinth in 146 B.C., that Hellenic culture began to flow
into the West.[26] Rome, the new political power about to enter its
era of greatness, was exporting military strength and government,
and importing Greek culture. Its governors and its military law
ruled the surrounding nations, and brought back to Rome from
each expedition learned men and wagonloads of art treasures
from Greece. Athens, under the domination of Macedonia, and
then of Rome, had neither opportunity nor need for vigorous
oratory. And rhetoric, as well as interest in its theory, left the
Agora and went to take its new place in the Roman Forum.

Rome, up to the decline of the Republic in the later years
of the first century B.C., was virtually governed by the Senate. Its
six hundred members, usually former magistrates, deliberated
upon all matters of legislation, foreign affairs, and finance. In
making all the more important decisions, they had freedom to
rise and speak on almost any topic at almost any time.[27] So the
gift of oratory, and particularly the gift of refined, Latin, oratorical style, became the most prized talent of those who wished to
wield legislative or judicial power in the Senate or in the courts
of Rome.

It is this refinement of style that is the contribution of Rome
and the specific contribution of Cicero to the development of
rhetoric. Cicero's rhetoric was not the fruit of a new philosophic

[26] *A Companion to Greek Studies*, ed. Leonard Whibley (4th ed. rev.;
London: Cambridge University Press, 1931), pp. 108 and 108–116.

[27] *A Companion to Latin Studies*, ed. John E. Sandys (3rd ed.; London: Cambridge University Press, 1935), pp. 283–284 and 290–291.

synthesis. Its basic philosophy was Aristotelian, with emphasis upon the truths Aristotle had inherited from his teacher, Plato.[28] He deals with no philosophical concepts in his rhetorical works and contents himself with a strong plea for the use of such concepts in preparing and educating young orators.[29]

Cicero's rhetoric is to be found in six works: De Inventione (86 B.C.), De Oratore (55 B.C.), Partitiones Oratoriae (54 B.C.), Orator (46 B.C.), De Optimo Genere Oratorum (46 B.C.), and Topica (44 B.C.). His definition of rhetoric seems best rendered in Baldwin's translation:

. . . he, methinks, is an orator, worthy of so responsible a title, who will say whatever falls to him for presentation, with wise forecast of the whole, order, style, memory, and a certain dignity of delivery.[30]

Both the author of the Rhetorica ad Herennium (about 86 B.C.), and Dionysius of Halicarnassus (De Compositione Verborum, about 20 B.C.), produced technical training manuals but they concerned themselves almost entirely with elements of style.[31]

Quintilian, on the other hand, had a definite effect upon the development of rhetoric because it was he who concentrated on how it was to be taught rather than on how it was to be practiced.[32] His classroom methods, gleaned from his monumental work, Institutio Oratoria (89 A.D.), were largely incorporated into the methodology of teaching the classics in the later ages of the seven liberal arts. He defines rhetoric as "the science of speaking well."[33] Any thorough scrutiny of his major work, however, will

[28] Mahaffy, op. cit., Vol. I, pp. 401–402.

[29] M. Tulli Ciceronis, De Oratore, ed. E. P. Crowell (Philadelphia: Eldredge & Brother, 1879), iii, 16.

[30] Charles S. Baldwin, Ancient Rhetoric and Poetic (New York: The Macmillan Company, 1924), p. 42.

[31] Wilmer C. Wright, A Short History of Greek Literature (New York: American Book Company, 1907), pp. 474–477.

[32] Thonssen and Baird, op. cit., pp. 91–93.

[33] Quintilianus, Institutio Oratoria, trans. H. E. Butler (Cambridge, Mass.: Harvard University Press, 1935), ii, 15, p. 317.

indicate clearly that his interests lay not with the deeper, philosophical concerns of rhetoric, but with how it should be taught in a classroom.

Meanwhile the oratory practiced outside the classroom had become so superficial and so vain that it was criticized bitterly by two of Quintilian's contemporaries—Tacitus, in the *Dialogus de Oratoribus* (80 A.D.),[34] and Petronius, in the *Satyricon*[35] (some time during the first century A.D.).

The Asianist tendencies to floridity and word manipulation perdured from Quintilian's time in the first century until the fifth century, long after the breakup of the Empire.[36] The now well-organized Christian church gave an impetus to sacred oratory. St. Augustine, writing his *Doctrina Christiana*[37] as a guide to sacred orators, at this time allowed himself little or no space for discussion of a philosophy of rhetoric. But it must be remembered that philosophy was taught along with rhetoric in the clerical schools as it had been in the Academy at Athens in classical times. And his work does give space to interpretation and, as such, is possibly the first work to touch expressly, though briefly, upon semantics.

Perhaps the most important development in rhetorical theory during this whole period came from the efforts of Capella, Cassiodore, and Isodore. Because of their planning and practice in monastic schools rhetoric was given a place among the seven liberal arts.[38]

Other medieval scholars like John of Salisbury (*Metalo-*

---

[34] The whole dialogue, but particularly paragraph 35, deplores these current sophistic tendencies. See P. Cornelius Tacitus, *Dialogus de Oratoribus*, ed. Alfred Gudeman (Boston: Ginn & Company, 1894).

[35] Thonssen and Baird, *op. cit.*, pp. 99–100.

[36] Baldwin, *op. cit.*, pp. 100–101.

[37] Thonssen and Baird, *op. cit.*, pp. 110–113.

[38] *Ibid.*, p. 110; and *A Companion to Latin Studies*, ed. John E. Sandys, p. 691.

gicus, 1159)[39] and Vincent of Beauvais (*Speculum Maius,* about the same time)[40] defended the place of rhetoric in the liberal arts and provided textbooks for its study.

With the sixteenth century came the discovery of the new world, the invention of practicable printing presses, and revolutions of a religious, social, and economic nature. Such an upheaval was bound to make the common man more vocal and individualistic, and there was enough to be vocal about in this busy age to inject new and vibrant life into the practice of rhetoric.

In the early days of this period of upheaval men like Melancthon (*Institutiones Rhetoricae,* 1521), Leonard Cox (*Arte or Crafte of Rhetoryke,* 1530), and Richard Sherry (*Treatise of Schemes and Tropes,* 1550) did little but reorganize the traditional ideas of Aristotelian theory with the Ciceronian emphasis upon style.[41] Thomas Wilson provided a more important work (*Arte of Rhetorique,* 1553) that succeeded in synthesizing all the classical principles and rules of rhetoric in one well-ordered text.[42] His emphasis on the end of rhetoric did, however, favor attention rather than the Aristotelian persuasion.[43]

About this same time, across the English Channel, Peter Ramus (Pierre La Ramée), with the help of his colleague, Omer Talon, was writing his *Dialecticae Libri Duo* (published in 1555). His opinion was that rhetoric should have nothing whatever to do with argumentation which was the business of logic alone. It should comprise only style and delivery, leaving invention, argumentation, and all else to logic.[44] The enthusiasm for these Ramist innovations in the classical trivium lasted until the middle of the seventeenth century.[45] Among the most important

---

[39] Thonssen and Baird, *op. cit.,* p. 114.
[40] Howell, *op. cit.,* pp. 76–78.
[41] *Ibid.,* pp. 92 and 90–95.   [43] *Ibid.,* pp. 98–110.
[42] Thonssen and Baird, *op. cit.,* p. 117.
[44] Howell, *op. cit.,* pp. 146–172.   [45] *Ibid.,* p. 280.

The Background of Rhetoric

enthusiasts were Gabriel Harvey, William Kempe, Dudley Fen-
ner, Abraham Fraunce, and Charles Butler.[46] But by 1625
Thomas Farnaby had published his *Index Rhetoricus* as the
spearhead of a neo-Ciceronian movement that brought back the
classical division of labors for rhetoric and logic.[47]

Meanwhile, the philosophic and scientific revolution of the
times was producing tendencies that were to change the conception of rhetoric if not its philosophy. In 1637 Descartes published his *Discours sur la Méthode,* setting up a new method of
philosophic inquiry which was to be applied eventually to science,
and was destined to change the whole conception of the duties
of logic and rhetoric.[48] Up to this time logic had been the means
of communicating learned discourse and rhetoric had limited itself to the role of communicating popular discourse. But now
logic became the instrument of inquiry and rhetoric took on the
office of communicating both learned and popular discourse.[49]
Francis Bacon's *The Advancement of Learning,* published in
1605, did much to promote this new, learned role of rhetoric. By
rhetoric, he seems to have meant simply communication. With
the work of Descartes and Bacon, rhetoric was not only given the
new duty of communicating learned information, but in line with
this new duty it was faced with the necessity of changing large
emphases in its structure. The Ramist and neo-Classical rhetoric
was far too decorative, too dependent upon emotional play, verbal
figures, and organizational tricks, to be useful for the communication of scientific ideas. So it had to adapt for itself a simpler, more
direct vocabulary and word order and a simpler style more akin
to ordinary discourse.[50] Two contemporary thinkers, Thomas
Hobbes (*A Briefe Art of Rhetorique,* 1637) and Bernard Lamy
(*The Art of Speaking,* 1688), championed this new simplicity of
style.[51]

[46] *Ibid.,* pp. 247–248 and 255–272. [47] *Ibid.,* pp. 318–322.
[48] *Ibid.,* p. 343. [49] *Ibid.,* pp. 364–365 and 386.
[50] *Ibid.,* pp. 364–375. [51] *Ibid.,* pp. 304–388 and 379–381.

In 1776, George Campbell wrote *The Philosophy of Rhetoric,* the most important work in rhetorical theory to appear since Wilson's work more than two hundred years earlier. He revived the Aristotelian emphasis upon audience response but dropped the use of deductive reasoning in argumentation for the inductive reasoning favored by Bacon and others.[52] Although his work does not treat all the elements usually considered in a full philosophy of rhetoric, he did concern himself more than anyone before him with the problems of interpretation and ambiguity which fall into the classification of word–thought–thing relationships or of definition. In fact, he devoted two large sections of his book to these philosophical problems.[53] Hugh Blair's *Lectures on Rhetoric,* appearing in 1783, took no new departures in the elements of rhetorical theory. The publication of Richard Whateley's *Rhetoric* in 1828 seems to have signaled a partial return to the more oratorical aspects of rhetoric and emphasized the old Aristotelian argumentation in a new organization. Beyond this attempt to simplify the old modes of argumentation, Whateley contributed heavily to the simplification of vocabulary and treatment of oratorical composition by championing the "natural manner" for speakers.[54]

With few exceptions of any moment in rhetorical theory, Whateley was the last rhetorician until the nineteen-twenties. John Bascom published a *Philosophy of Rhetoric* in 1885 in the midst of a general decline of interest in rhetoric. In America the standard textbooks of Blair and Campbell were widely used until, toward the end of the nineteenth century, it became the aim of rhetoric courses to teach young people the "correct" grammar that was then so much more necessary for social acceptance.

[52] Thonssen and Baird, *op. cit.,* p. 137.

[53] George Campbell, *The Philosophy of Rhetoric* (Boston: J. H. Wilkins & Co., Hilliard, Gray, and Co., and Gould, Lincoln, and Kendall, 1835).

[54] Thonssen and Baird, *op. cit.,* pp. 217, 139–143, and 140–143.

THE TRADITIONAL THEORY OF RHETORIC

If one thing is evident from the foregoing sketch of the history of rhetoric, it is that the philosophy of rhetoric has not perceptibly changed since Aristotle. Even the new epistemologies of the later English, German, and French philosophers had little effect on rhetoric as they found no application in the field of rhetorical theory. A description of the philosophy of rhetoric, as it finds itself on the advent of the three new theories to be analyzed in this volume—a description, really, of the four Aristotelian philosophical elements most basic to rhetoric—is here most pertinent. These four elements will be described briefly as: thought–word–thing relationships, abstraction, definition, and argumentation.

Aristotle's consideration of *thought–word–thing relationships* is in the treatise "De Anima" and the "Metaphysica,"[55] although the consideration of real objects and their nature is also discussed in the "Physica."[56] First of all, things which are perceivable to the senses are real. They are not just projections of the mind, but actually and physically exist independently of whether the mind is thinking of them or not.[57] Next, the way these real things are known, experienced, perceived, or conceived, depends upon the capacities of the knowing subject.[58] Man, for Aristotle as for philosophers, has all the capacities of the lower forms of life, as well as his own specific capacities of intellectual judgment

[55] *The Basic Works of Aristotle*, "De Anima," ii, 5–6, pp. 565–567 (417*a*–418*a*); iii, 3–8, pp. 586–596 (427*b*–432*a*); "Metaphysica," i, 1, pp. 689–691 (980*a*–982*a*); iii, 2, pp. 720–722 (997*b*–998*b*); iii, 4, pp. 724–725 (999*a*–1000*a*); iii, 5, pp. 729–731 (1001*b*–1002*b*); and vii, 12–14, pp. 803–807 (1037*b*–1039*b*).

[56] *Ibid.*, "Physica," pp. 218–394 (184*a*–267*b*).

[57] The whole tenor of Aristotle's discussion in "De Anima" and in the "Physica" is based upon and implies the extensional, physical reality of entities outside the mind.

[58] *The Basic Works of Aristotle*, "De Anima," iii, 3–5, pp. 586–592 (427*b*–430*a*).

and volitional decision. Thus his elementary perceptions, at least
in initial stages, can be similar to the lowest animal perceptions
of, for instance, heat, cold, pressure, movement, and the like.[59]
This perception is, of course, vague and unformed and can be
considered roughly similar to what William James called "primordial abstraction."[60] But human thought and its processes require, for Aristotle, the making of an entirely new kind of entity,
different from the soul which is intellectual, spiritual, nonmaterial, and yet different as well from physical reality which is often
measurable and material. When the mind (soul, psyche) knows
a physical thing, it knows it through the senses with a kind of animal perception.[61] When the image (form, species, idea, thought)
of the thing gets into the mind, it takes on the characteristics of
the mind. It has to be nonmaterial, spiritual, and intellectual, because it has become a phase or activity of the intellect or spirit.
This is the idea or thought or form.[62] The thought, then, is not
just matter, because it is a spiritual activity. It is not spiritual activity alone, because it carries the form, or is the form, of a real,
measurable, physical thing. So it has to be a new kind of halfway
entity between real things and spiritual activity, a new entity, half
body, half spirit. The new entity is the metaphysical thing or
being.[63] It is an idea, a thought, but it has its roots in physical
things. It has reality because it can be in one mind independently
of the activity of other minds. It has spirituality because it is the
activity of a spiritual capacity. Even abstractions are real in this
metaphysical sense, so long as the things they are abstracted
from are real.[64] These two kinds of reality, physical and meta-

[59] *Ibid.*, ii, 3–5, pp. 559–567 (414b–418a).
[60] *Ibid.*, "Analytica Posteriora," ii, 19, pp. 184–186 (99b–100b); and
William James, *Psychology* (New York: Henry Holt and Co., Inc., c1892),
pp. 7–27 and 239–243.
[61] *Ibid.*, "De Anima," ii, 3, pp. 559–560 (414b–415a).
[62] *Ibid.*, iii, 7, p. 595 (431b–432a).
[63] *Ibid.*, iii, 4–5, pp. 590–593 (429b–430b); and iii, 3–9, pp. 589–596
(429a–432b).
[64] *Ibid.*, "Analytica Posteriora," i, 11, pp. 125–126 (44a).

physical, are important to Aristotle, because reality is the criterion of certainty and truth. An idea, a judgment, even a complete argumentation, is true only to the extent that such an idea or judgment or argumentation corresponds with reality independent of the mind.[65]

Aristotle's theory of *abstraction* follows the thought–word–thing relationships very closely. Indeed, it is in treating of the thought process in "De Anima," the "Metaphysica," and the "Analytica Posteriora," that he implies what he means by abstraction.[66] When a mind thinks of something that is not concrete and individual, when it begins to compare the thought of a cloud, for instance, with the thought of a piece of paper or a puff of smoke, it immediately begins to sort out the characteristics of things and range them together with complete unconcern as to whether this can be done extensively and physically outside the mind or not.[67] It can classify cloud and smoke under puffiness, or it can classify cloud and paper under whiteness. It can and does go on endlessly making such classifications. All of them require abstractions. This is, of course, what most philosophers have always agreed upon as intellectual abstraction. The psychological surgery of selecting and classifying the physically inseparable elements and phases of things is foundational to the human power to judge, to choose, and to measure. Eventually, for the orator and the writer, it be-

---

[65] René Descartes, *Discours de la Méthode*, with introduction and notes by Etienne Gilson (Paris: J. Vrin, 1935). Descartes's work undermined, for many, the Aristotelian criterion of truth. Locke, Berkeley, and Hume, among others, questioned the Aristotelian epistemology with their inquiries into the mind's objectivizing activities. But none of this seems to have been felt in rhetoric theory or teaching practice. See Edwin A. Burtt (ed.), *The English Philosophers from Bacon to Mill* (New York: Random House, Inc., 1939), Introduction, pp. xix–xxi.

[66] *The Basic Works of Aristotle*, "De Anima," iii, 4, pp. 589–596 (429*a*–432*b*); "Metaphysica," i, 1, pp. 689–690 (980*a*–981*b*); "Analytica Posteriora," i, 11, pp. 125–126 (77*a*).

[67] *Ibid.*, "Analytica Posteriora," ii, 19, pp. 184–186 (99*b*–100*b*).

comes the power to guide or help others to judge, choose, and measure facts and probabilities.

Furthermore, for Aristotle, the abstractive process is clearly basic to any proposition or statement that is predicative. When the predicate of a sentence says that something belongs to the subject, as it usually does, then there is an abstractive classification involved.[68] The statement "John is honest" involves a process whereby the abstracted characteristic of honesty is predicated of John. The mind has already experienced hundreds of subjects who possess this characteristic of honesty. It has abstracted this one characteristic and known it as precised or set apart from the other qualities in the hundreds of subjects. It has even returned to classify all the hundreds of subjects as being in the "honest" class. Now it sees and knows one more subject, John, and predicates the abstracted characteristic of him, too. This situation and its abstractive classifying process is not limited to "is" propositions, so expressed. Other predicative propositions are easily reducible to this simple form. "John works hard" involves the same abstractive classifying process. It reduces to the predicative "is" by simply reforming itself to say "John is one who works hard." Tense, mood, and voice do not, of course, affect this process, nor do they affect the reducibility of the proposition so long as it is a predicative proposition. Since most of the statements made in a rhetorical unit are predicative in this way,[69] it becomes clear that abstraction theory is at the heart of the study of rhetoric.

Aristotle's theory of *definition* is found principally in the "Categoriae"[70] and the "Analytica Posteriora."[71] From his con-

[68] *Ibid.*, i, 11, pp. 125–126 (77a).

[69] *Ibid.*, i, 4, pp. 115–119 (73a–74b). This explains Aristotle's kinds of logical predication. The "accidental" type also certainly applies to rhetoric, but always with the precaution, noted in "Rhetorica," i, 2, pp. 1331–1333 (1357a–1357b), that the business of rhetoric is not with certainties but with probabilities.

[70] *Ibid.*, "Categoriae," v, pp. 9–14 (2a–4b).

[71] *Ibid.*, "Analytica Posteriora," ii, 19, pp. 184–186 (99b–100b).

siderations of thought–word–thing relationships, Aristotle had concluded that he could have true thoughts. The mind could think with truth about clouds or paper or whiteness or puffiness. With its abstractive capacity, the mind could separate, mentally, the puffiness of the cloud from the flat, hard whiteness of the paper. Since it could make such distinctions with the aid of the senses, it could also assemble thoughts which could designate a physically real or metaphysically real thing without having to point to it to make clear which exact thing was meant.[72] In this way, Aristotle, at the Academy, might refer to a real thing by saying, for instance, "Socrates' trial." This would refer to a real, sensible entity but one that was easily distinguishable from other real, sensible entities like the market place of Sparta, or the recent wind storm. It was also easily distinguishable from other trials, since this was the one where Socrates was tried. This is, in a way, defining things. But for more metaphysical things, so much more commonly used in discussions at the Academy, he used what he called definition by "genus" and "species."[73] Though not essentially different from the delineating method used to indicate Socrates' trial, this type of defining meant that, for a thing or a thought, its general class or "genus" had to be pointed out and then its "species" or what special kind of a thought or thing it was. The thought "man," then, abstract and metaphysical as it was, could be defined by signifying man's "genus," that is, "animal," and his "species," that is, "rational." Thus, for Aristotle and Aristotelians, man is defined validly and scientifically as

[72] Aristotle's treatment of *definition* in Book ii of the "Analytica Posteriora" is only meant in his strict sense of essential genus and species. But his types of definition in ii, 10, pp. 169–170 (93*b*–94*a*), as well as the transition from logic to rhetoric, from proof and certainty to opinion and probability, in the "Rhetorica," i, 2, p. 1330 (1356*b*), make it reasonable to infer that Aristotle also intended, for ordinary purposes, what is generally called descriptive or designative definition. For Aristotle, however, strict definition was a statement of the essence of a thing and not primarily a way to distinguish it individually from other things. See "Metaphysica," iii, 2, p. 718 (996*b*).

[73] *The Basic Works of Aristotle*, "Categoriae," iii, p. 8 (1*b*).

a rational animal.[74] Whenever, for more practical and conversational uses, the definer needs more details to distinguish and
designate a more concrete thing, he can still use these classifications or others more specific.[75] As an example, "Athenians who
go to the baths at sunrise" would signify a class, but a more de-
terminate and limited class than the genus–species definition can
adequately designate. Defining, even in this case, is a question of
signifying the general, or relatively general, class and adding
some detail that makes it easier to pick out the thing defined, or
de-limited or *de*-scribed.

The traditional *argumentation* comes from the logic to be
found in the six treatises of Aristotle in the "Organon." Even
though the inductive type of logic was less emphasized by him,
it is treated fully here[76] and later applied to rhetoric in the same
manner as is deduction.[77] While Aristotle is careful to point out
the difference between rhetorical argument and logical proof,
careful to concede that while logic should lead to certainties and
argumentation in rhetoric should lead to opinions, still the processes of arriving at both kinds of conclusion are based upon the
same reasoning operations.[78] The logical form of valid propositions of various kinds and the syllogistic process of combining two
terms with a middle term to produce a new propositional truth
is the same. In rhetoric, however, this syllogistic process is made
informal. The middle term is simply appended to the concluding
proposition by way of a reason why it ought to be true. In the
logic,[79] an Aristotelian syllogism might read:

[74] *Ibid.,* v, p. 9 (2*a*–2*b*).
[75] This seems to follow from man's power to abstract and classify. His
power can be applied to nonessential elements of things as well as to essentials. See "Metaphysica," viii, 2, pp. 814–817 (1043*a*–1043*b*); and "Categoriae," v, pp. 9–14 (2*a*–5*a*).
[76] *Ibid.,* "Analytica Priora," ii, 23–24, pp. 102–103 (68*b*–69*a*); and
"Analytica Posteriora," ii, 1, pp. 158–159 (89*b*).
[77] *Ibid.,* "Rhetorica," ii, 20, pp. 1412–1414 (1393*b*–1394*a*).
[78] *Ibid.,* i, 2, p. 1332 (1357*a*–1357*b*).
[79] *Ibid.,* "Analytica Posteriora," i, 6, pp. 118–121 (74*b*–75*a*).

Whatever has no parts is simple.	(Major premise)
The soul has no parts.	(Minor premise)
The soul, therefore, is simple.	(Conclusion)

In rhetoric the middle term, "having no parts," is just given with the conclusion as a reason for so concluding. It would read: "The soul is simple because it has no parts." Or, more properly in accord with the opinion content of rhetorical conclusions, another example might be better: "Candidate Smith will make the best mayor because he is the most honest politician in town." This informal and collapsed syllogism Aristotle called an "enthymeme."[80] He informalized the inductive kind of reasoning by the device of the example, as a specific and real instance where what was being argued was true.[81]

Against this background of history and of the traditional rhetorical theory, it should be easier to appreciate the three new theories that are treated in the succeeding pages.

[80] *Ibid.*, "Rhetorica," i, 2, pp. 1330–1334 (1356*b*–1358*a*).
[81] *Ibid.*, ii, 20, pp. 1412–1413 (1393*b*–1394*a*).

CHAPTER 2

I. A. Richards' Theory

THE WORK OF PROFESSOR I. A. RICHARDS PRESENTS A SUBSTANTIAL departure from the traditional theory of rhetoric. He does not start his inquiry into rhetoric with a metaphysical methodology, as did Aristotle. He starts with the psychobiological origins of man's drive to express himself in linguistic and other symbols. His method of inquiry, too, as he has explained it to the writer, is Platonic and dialectical, rather than Aristotelian and organizational. Plato's idea structure shows also in Richards' near-nominalistic relations between thoughts and things. There are three major additional differences that mark Richards' rhetoric as new. (1) He uses the findings of modern biology and psychology to help him explain the functions of rhetorical language. (2) He regards metaphor as a central aspect of rhetoric. (3) He deals with rhetoric not only as speech but as part of the communication process, whether a person is speaking, listening, writing, or reading to achieve efficient comprehension. These characteristics will, it is hoped, become clear in the delineation of Richards' theory that follows.

The treatment of Richards' theory is divided into six sections: his background and approach to rhetoric; his theory of

28

abstraction; his approach to metaphor; his conception of thought–word–thing relationships; his theory of definition; and his theory of comprehending.

THE BACKGROUND AND APPROACH TO RHETORIC

Education at Cambridge University and five subsequent years there as a colleague of C. K. Ogden led to Richards' co-authorship with Ogden in his first important work connected with rhetorical theory, *The Meaning of Meaning* (1923). His research and reading since that time make him a recognized scholar in many relevant fields. Following *The Meaning of Meaning,* he published *Principles of Literary Criticism* (1924) and *Science and Poetry* (1925). Then, still at Cambridge, he published the results of his experiments with comprehension in *Practical Criticism* (1929). These works, all leaning toward a theory of interpretation, were written while Richards worked with Ogden on a basic English vocabulary that would simplify the problems of the translator and the beginner learning the English language. The next year, spent as visiting professor at Tsing Hua University in Peking, not only gave Richards experience with problems of interpretation, but seems to have confirmed his early theory. On his return from the East and while visiting Harvard, he published the results of his Peking studies in *Mencius on the Mind* (1931). The next four years saw three works into print. *Basic Rules of Reason* (1933) and *Coleridge on Imagination* (1934) testify to his persevering interest in the functions of the mind, relative to language. *The Philosophy of Rhetoric* (1936) is a series of lectures on Richards' new conception of rhetoric.

A second visit to Peking, from 1936 to 1938, as Director of the Orthological Institute of China, gave him time to get into publication the results of another set of experiments in interpretation. *Interpretation in Teaching* (1938), prepared for teachers, attempted to apply his theory of interpretation to the classroom.

Subsequently he returned to Harvard University and served as Director of the Harvard Commission on English Language Studies, from 1939 to 1944, and from 1944 to the present as Director of Language Research. All this experience in the meaning aspects of language must have had a bearing on the final cast of his theory of rhetoric so directly aimed, as it is, at comprehension of meaning. These later years have provided educators and teachers with the most recent and mature formulation of Richards' work. In a letter commenting on the present analysis of his theory, he says:

I feel that my later work—with the deep indebtedness to Coleridge and Plato—is likely to be of far more permanent interest than the earlier (with its echoes, via Ogden mainly, of Bentham).[1]

Among other works, the most pertinent to rhetoric in these later years are *How to Read a Page* (1942) and *Speculative Instruments* (1955). The first makes much clearer the function of reason in the abstractive process. The latter contains one chapter that concisely explains what all the other works have been leading up to—his theory of comprehending.

In the wide range of his scholarly publications, the depth of his research in the many fields related to rhetoric stands out. He seems as familiar with Socrates as with Russell, as well read in logic and the mathematics of communication as in linguistics and psychology. Stanley Hyman says:

His learning in almost every area of knowledge is so tremendous, his significance so great in half a dozen fields besides criticism, and the brilliance and subtlety of at least his earlier books so overpowering, that any hit-and-run treatment of him in a few thousand words is bound to be laughably superficial.[2]

In conversation with the writer, Richards has revealed his deep roots in Plato and Coleridge, and the influence of other

[1] Letter from I. A. Richards, Boston, December 7, 1956.
[2] Stanley E. Hyman, *The Armed Vision* (New York: Vintage Books, Inc., 1955), p. 278. c1947, 1948, 1955, by Alfred Knopf, Inc.

philosophers which is probably more prominent in his later works. He feels that whatever influence Kant and Bentham had on his work must have come through Ogden, and that a lot of his theory about thought–word–thing relationships might have come from the latter part of the "Analytica Posteriora" of Aristotle. Otherwise he acknowledges the help of G. F. Stout's psychology, Piaget's studies of children's language habits, and, for his first notions on primordial abstraction, William James's *Psychology*.[3] There are, however, strong Gestalt leanings[4] throughout his theory supplanting an admitted beginning in Associationism.[5] The preface to the first edition of *The Meaning of Meaning* testifies to the influence of Malinowski,[6] at least upon the contents of that early work.

It is important, for those interested in a practical teaching rhetoric, to remember that Richards is himself a teacher. Much of the research for his books was done in the classroom.[7] Whatever he may offer toward the improvement of courses in composition, speech, writing, and communication will be practical suggestions from a practicing teacher.

Richards' definition of rhetoric is borrowed from George Campbell's *The Philosophy of Rhetoric* (1835). For Campbell, rhetoric was the art of adapting discourse to its end.[8] The ap-

[3] Interview with I. A. Richards, Boston, October 5, 1956.

[4] Richards' theory of context is clearly Gestaltist, as is his conception of comparison fields in his most recent theory of comprehending.

[5] I. A. Richards, *The Philosophy of Rhetoric* (New York: Oxford University Press, c1936), p. 15.

[6] C. K. Ogden and I. A. Richards, *The Meaning of Meaning* (London: Routledge and Kegan Paul, Ltd., 1923), Preface to 1st ed., p. lx. Originally published by Harcourt, Brace & Co., Inc., New York.

[7] Two of Richards' books are the direct result of classroom experiments: *Practical Criticism* (New York: Harcourt, Brace & Co., Inc., c1929) and *Interpretation in Teaching* (New York: Harcourt, Brace & Co., Inc., c1938).

[8] George Campbell, *The Philosophy of Rhetoric* (Boston: J. H. Wilkins and Co., Hilliard, Gray, and Co., and Gould, Lincoln, and Kendall, 1835), p. 11.

proach that brought Richards to this conception of a teaching rhetoric is Platonic rather than Aristotelian, as we have said. Richards does not build upon a foundation with logical blocks, from the ground up. His schematic idea of methodology is to start with whatever sticks up as the most urgent and pertinent element of a problem, and then work in any direction at all that has the scent of truth. The important thing, seemingly, to Richards, is to be free to seek in any direction at any time.[9] As he narrates the progressive steps in his early studies in rhetoric, this organismic rather than architectural method of inquiry becomes clear.

His point of departure was the most urgent and obvious question about man. What is the symbol-using power that is uniquely characteristic of him? Beginning with what was observable, Richards turned to the findings of biology and psychology. He could see that man shared with the most elemental types of animal the stimulus and response patterns of the merely nutritive and sense life. The response of an amoeba to prodding or the directional growing of a vine is not essentially different from the blinking of a man's eyes in a sudden strong light or the thrusting out of his hands as he begins to fall. Viewing such phenomena of response in the light of modern biology and psychology, Richards could describe them as fundamental sorting of the things they experienced.[10] Responses of organisms could be classified into two rough categories: acceptance and rejection. Repeated and multiplied experience conditioned the sortings into the habits of growth and feeding we observe.[11]

But man, besides the responses he shares with these ele-

[9] Richards quotes from Plato's "Republic" to illustrate this dialectic seeking of the truth. He illustrates it himself in his inquiry steps from elemental biological abstraction to conceptual abstraction, to epistemology. For dialectic inquiry method, see *How to Read a Page* (New York: W. W. Norton & Company, Inc., 1942), pp. 215–222.

[10] Ogden and Richards, *op. cit.*, p. 8; also Richards, *The Philosophy of Rhetoric*, pp. 29–31.

[11] Richards, *The Philosophy of Rhetoric*, p. 30.

mental animals, has a unique kind of response to stimuli of all kinds, elemental or otherwise. He can use language symbols to express his feelings and needs. He even has a special way of assimilating and integrating with exterior stimuli.[12] He experiences what we call thoughts about these stimuli. Somehow, within his own organism, he can know what he is sorting from what, and make comparisons. Furthermore, he can store away residual traces of his sorting experiences in such a way that he can call them up again and again at will, without the original stimulus being there at all. So man is constantly comparing new experiences with old ones, in search of similarity.[13] At this point Richards seems to have seen that classifying with this conceptual sorting facility means distinguishing things from one another by abstract characteristics. Thus, out of primordial abstraction, or elementary animal sorting, he came to conceptual abstraction. As Richards explains:

A sensation would be something that was just *so*, on its own, a datum; as such we have none. Instead we have perceptions, responses whose character comes to them from the past as well as the present occasion. A perception is never just of an *it*; perception takes whatever it perceives as a thing of a certain sort. All thinking from the lowest to the highest—whatever else it may be—is sorting.[14]

It will help to remember, as we proceed with the discussion of abstraction and metaphor, thought–word–thing relationships and definition, that these four philosophical elements are probably equally basic and quite inseparable except for the purpose of discussion. Abstraction and epistemology and definition elements certainly do imply and include one another. Here we separate them only mentally, and we begin with abstraction only because it follows so naturally from Richards' starting point in primordial sorting.

---

[12] *Ibid.*   [13] Ogden and Richards, *op. cit.*, p. 52.
[14] Richards, *The Philosophy of Rhetoric*, p. 30.

THE THEORY OF ABSTRACTION

In general, an abstraction is for Richards what it has been to philosophers for centuries: the selection of a characteristic attributable to many real objects, its segregation in the mind as an abstract idea, and its expression in symbols as an abstract word.[15]

But biology and psychology gave Richards insights into the process of abstracting. One of these insights involves his concept of the ἀρχή (reason). The other involves his notion of context.

The ἀρχή notion follows from primordial sorting. Since man possesses the characteristic abilities of each of the animal forms from the simplest to the most complex, he can put all these abilities to work in reaction to a given stimulus. His response can be, at one and the same time, biological, emotional, and conceptual.[16] When he does conceptualize a response, he can express it in language symbols. There is a complexity here, because the biological, emotional, and conceptual elements in the response fight for dominance at one another's expense.[17] There is a risk, then, of loss of real meaning in the expression of the real happening in language symbols. The organism sorts and compares the experience with other similar past experiences. When it conceptualizes the experience, when it abstracts the characteristic it selects (as it must do to classify it), it may be abstracting an emotional aspect and neglecting a very important conceptual meaning.[18] For example, catching a quick glimpse of a large red glow at the stage end of a theatre might call up past similar experiences of glowing red. One could recall the flame that once burned his finger, or a harrowing experience in a flaming building. He might, in instinctive panic, shout, "Fire!" If he did, he would have selected

[15] Ogden and Richards, *op. cit.*, pp. 213–214; and Richards, *The Philosophy of Rhetoric*, p. 31.

[16] Ogden and Richards, *op. cit.*, pp. 223–225; Richards, *The Philosophy of Rhetoric*, pp. 40–41; and *How to Read a Page*, pp. 98–99.

[17] Richards, *How to Read a Page*, p. 75.

[18] Ogden and Richards, *op. cit.*, pp. 124–125.

34

the emotionally frightening element of his own experience to interpret what might, on further examination, be only a red stage light for dramatic effect.

Richards' answer to this complexity of choice in the abstractive process is the ἀρχή (reason) whose function it is to control both the emotional and the conceptual elements in the process in a way that ensures the proper, realistic, and balanced whole meaning of the event. It is under the guidance and control of the reason that the process of abstraction can produce true and realistic abstract symbols.[19]

Richards' other important insight into the abstraction process is as closely connected with meaning as the first. He refers to the term "context" in a special sense. It includes not only all the concomitant surroundings of a thought and of the event the thought is about, but the whole complex of similar thoughts and events that might be compared with it in the mind's sortings. In short, a context embraces the whole field of experience that can be connected with an experienced event, or with the thought of that event.[20]

When we abstract, of course, we select some element from a very intricate maze of contexts, all classified under multiple aspects of past abstractions, like a complicated cross-reference index system.[21] When we abstract the characteristic "red" and apply it to the stage of a theatre, we have selected "red" from thousands of contexts, ranging through fire engines to the flush that accompanies embarrassment. The ἀρχή may have managed to control and balance the emotional elements in these contexts with the conceptual elements, and prevented our jumping to the untrue abstractive judgment that the stage is on fire. But there is another complexity here. The abstraction in any given event to be expressed has its own context, made up of the con-

[19] Richards, *How to Read a Page*, pp. 74–75 and 101–102.

[20] Ogden and Richards, *op. cit.*, pp. 56–58; and Richards, *The Philosophy of Rhetoric*, pp. 34–37.

[21] *Ibid.*, p. 35.

comitant external and internal, real and remembered elements
that connect with the thought and symbol "red" in this theatre,
for this person, at this time.[22] Now the term "red" selects only the
color characteristic and leaves out all the rest of the richness of
the context. For the full meaning of "red," we have to look to the
whole context of the symbol. From the concept of abstraction,
Richards has come to the nature of meaning. In this connection
he says:

> In these contexts one item—typically a word—takes over the duties of
> parts which can then be omitted from the recurrence. There is thus
> an abridgement of the context only shown in the behavior of living
> things, and most extensively and drastically shown by man. When
> this abridgement happens, what the sign or word—the item with
> these delegated powers—means is the missing parts of the context.[23]

Richards' final admonition about abstraction is that we
should remember it as a mental activity, and valid only in that
sense.[24] In the discussion of parts of context and the conflict between emotion and intellect, we tend to think of these elements
as really separate and distinct. This is one of the liabilities of
abstraction. The parts of the context are one, and the desiring of
the emotions is never quite separable from the thinking of the
intellect. As Richards puts it, "We cannot, in fact, wholly leave
off wanting. No thinking can be motiveless."[25]

We can proceed now, quite naturally, from Richards' general
theory of abstraction to his most important application of it in the
theory of metaphor.

AN APPROACH TO METAPHOR

The analysis that Richards makes of metaphor harks back
to his theory of abstraction. All metaphor does, after all, is ab-

[22] Ogden and Richards, *op. cit.*, p. 56.
[23] Richards, *The Philosophy of Rhetoric*, p. 34.
[24] Richards, *How to Read a Page*, pp. 98–99.   [25] *Ibid.*, p. 99.

stract from one reference (thought) and attribute the abstracted quality of another reference for the purpose of clarifying or livening up its meaning. [26] Take, for example, the metaphor in the utterance "He was a lion in battle." Here are two symbols, "lion" and "man," and two references (thoughts), one for the lion and one for the man. The "lion" reference has been selected by the communicator as suitable to clarify or enliven his communicated reference of the man as a courageous fighter. Abstraction is the process used to select from the "lion" reference the characteristic of courage as being the most appropriate one among all the elements and characteristics in all the "lion" contexts usually known to people. Having eliminated all the other characteristics of "lion" and all the rest of their contexts, the communicator welded the abstracted quality of courage to the other reference, "man." It is this welding, this borrowing of a characteristic from one reference to attach it to another, that is essential to metaphor-making and distinguishes it from ordinary abstraction.[27] Richards sums up this theory in *The Philosophy of Rhetoric*:

In the simplest formulation, when we use a metaphor we have two thoughts of different things active together and supported by a single word, or phrase, whose meaning is a resultant of the interaction.[28]

For use in the discussion of metaphor, Richards has introduced two new terms, which, for him, avoid the ambiguity of the traditional terminology of metaphor. The term "tenor" he applies to the "underlying idea or principal subject which the vehicle or figure means."[29] This is the man in the example, "He was a lion in battle." The term "vehicle" is attached to the other reference—"lion"—that lends its selected characteristics to make the tenor clearer or more vivid.[30] For the basis of relationship between the

---

[26] Ogden and Richards, *op. cit.*, p. 213.   [27] *Ibid.*, pp. 213–214.
[28] Richards, *The Philosophy of Rhetoric*, p. 93.
[29] *Ibid.*, p. 97.   [30] *Ibid.*, pp. 79 and 100.

two references or parts of the metaphor, he uses the traditional term "ground."[31]

Richards' most emphatic contention about metaphor, thus explained, is that language is naturally metaphoric. Since metaphor is just abstraction for the purpose of clearer and more vivid communication,[32] since it seems to be the nature of our thinking to be perpetually busy with sorting and classifying references and comparing contexts and their parts, and since our language symbolizes this thinking, it seems to Richards that our language must be highly, habitually, and even naturally metaphoric. He takes issue with Aristotle on this point in the early part of his treatment of metaphor in *The Philosophy of Rhetoric*.[33] Aristotle's contention seems to be that ability to use metaphor cannot be taught to another and that it is a sign of genius, inasmuch as it indicates an eye for resemblances. Richards' counter contention is, of course, that metaphor-making ability comes naturally to ordinary people. He remarks, in fact, that:

We cannot get through three sentences of ordinary fluid discourse without it. . . . Even in the rigid language of the settled sciences we do not eliminate or prevent it without great difficulty.[34]

Richards' theories of abstraction and metaphor have involved three elements of the thought process that need special examination. The next section will deal with Richards' concept of the relationships between thoughts, words, and things.

THOUGHT–WORD–THING RELATIONSHIPS

Richards' epistemological theory concerns itself a good deal more with the operations of thoughts (references), words (symbols), and things (referents) than with their nature. As he states his aim, it is to find out "how words work."[35] The foregoing ac-

[31] *Ibid.*, p. 117.   [32] Ogden and Richards, *op. cit.*, pp. 213–214.
[33] Richards, *The Philosophy of Rhetoric*, pp. 89–93.
[34] *Ibid.*, p. 92.   [35] *Ibid.*, pp. 8 and 23.

count of abstraction has shown how the thought process takes place, but has said nothing of the relationships between the three elements involved. The epistemological inquiry is, of course, not a distinct and different inquiry, but rather the same one viewed from a different angle.

At the outset there is need for a definition of Richards' terms. And possibly the best way to answer that need will be to cite his own description of the "match scrape" example of a mental operation and then cite his own definitions of all the elements in that exemplary operation:

The effects upon the organism due to any sign, which may be any stimulus from without, or any process taking place within, depend upon the past history of the organism, both generally and in more precise fashion. In a sense, no doubt, the whole past history is relevant; but there will be some among the past events in that history which will more directly determine the nature of the present agitation than others. Thus when we strike a match, the movements we make and the sound of the scrape are present stimuli. But the excitation which results is different from what it would be had we never struck matches before. Past strikings have left, in our organization, engrams, residual traces, which help to determine what the mental process will be. For instance the mental process is among other things an awareness that we are striking a *match*. Apart from the effects of similar previous situations we should have no such awareness. Suppose further that the awareness is accompanied by an expectation of a flame. The expectation again will be due to the effects of situations in which the striking of a match has been followed by a flame. The expectation is the excitation of part of an engram complex, which is called up by the stimulus (the scrape) similar to a part only of the original stimulus-situation.[36]

Here is a sign situation, a reference–symbol–referent unit —that is, a thought–word–thing unit—in which can be found all the elements for which Richards has specific terms. The *reference* is the thought about the scraping match and all its concomitant

[36] Ogden and Richards, *op. cit.*, p. 52. Originally published by Harcourt, Brace & Co., Inc., New York, and quoted with their permission.

elements, together with similar groups of elements remembered as past similar experiences.[37] The *symbol* would of course be any language unit used to express what has gone on in the example. "Match scrape," for instance, might express it in a given circumstance.[38] The *referent* is the actual event of the scraping of the match and the real concomitant motions, noises, sights, and so on, that happen independently of the subject's thought.[39] The *sign* is that one stimulus in the whole complex event which has the effect of reminding the subject of the rest of the details of the event as well as remembrances of past associable events—in this case, the scraping itself.[40] The *context* is the whole event with all its associations from the subject's past experience. Richards calls it a *psychological* context when referring to the event in thought process and linked with other, remembered, similar thought processes. He calls it an *external* context when referring to the actual event as happening outside the mind.[41] The movement of the fingers, the flash of light, and all the other concomitant real happenings of the match-scrape event are parts of the external context. The last important element in the sign situation is the *engram*. The term refers to the residual trace of some past excitation, either in the nerve tissue or in some other physiological function of a part of the organism.[42]

Richards' own definitions of these terms will serve to clarify the example and its explanation:

. . . for words, arrangements of words, images, gestures, and such representations as drawings or mimetic sounds we use the term symbols.[43]

. . . a reference . . . is a set of external and psychological contexts linking a mental process to a referent.[44]

. . . a referent . . . thing . . . object.[45]

[37] *Ibid.*, p. 90. [38] *Ibid.*, pp. 9 and 23. [39] *Ibid.*, p. 9, footnote.
[40] *Ibid.*, p. 53. [41] *Ibid.*, pp. 58, 56–57, and 263–265.
[42] *Ibid.*, p. 53. [43] *Ibid.*, p. 23. [44] *Ibid.*, p. 90.
[45] *Ibid.*, p. 9, footnote.

A sign is always a stimulus similar to some part of an original stimulus and sufficient to call up the engram formed by that stimulus.[46]

A context is a set of entities (things or events) related in a certain way; these entities have each a character such that other sets of entities occur having the same characters and related by the same relation; and these occur "nearly uniformly."[47]

An engram is the residual trace of an adaption made by the organism to a stimulus.[48]

With the match-scrape example and a definition of terms, it becomes easier to understand Richards' diagram[49] of the relationships between thought, word, and thing; between reference, symbol, and referent:

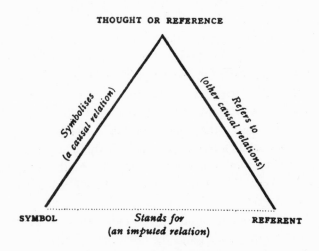

FIGURE 1—From *The Meaning of Meaning*, by C. K. Ogden and I. A. Richards (Routledge and Kegan Paul, Ltd., 1923), p. 11. Used by permission.

As can be seen in Richards' diagram, there is a causal relationship between the reference and the symbol. In other words,

[46] *Ibid.*, p. 53. [47] *Ibid.*, p. 58.
[48] *Ibid.*, p. 53. [49] *Ibid.*, p. 11.

the communicator using a certain word or expression can cause his hearers to form a thought somewhat similar to his own. And, conversely, the thought or reference can cause, at least in part, the use of a certain symbol to express it.

The second relationship, between the reference and the referent, is also causal, inasmuch as the thing, or referent, which is or has been seen, felt, heard, and so on, has stimulated the organism and caused it to think about the source of the stimulation or have a reference about it. This causation can be directly from the present stimulation or indirectly from past stimulations or the memory of such stimulations.

But the last relationship—and this is the important one for Richards—is not directly causal, nor is the relationship a real one in the sense of the other two. This "imputed" relationship points to the key principle from which stems Richards' theory of propositional truth, his value norms, his theory of definition, and the validity of his criteria for accurate interpretation. It is the principle stating that there is no referential relation between the symbol and the referent, between the word and the thing. To phrase it differently, the symbol, or word, does not really "refer to" the thing or referent except indirectly through the thought or reference. The symbol merely "stands for" the thing referred to by the reference. Whereas it symbolizes the reference, it does not symbolize the thing.[50]

This key contention about the indirectness of the relationship between the symbol and the referent is of major importance to Richards, because a failure to understand and apply it is, for him, at the root of most of the problems of conceptual meaning.[51] The confusions of ambiguity and word shifts, multiple meaning, and out-of-place definitions are, in his theory, at least partly ascribable to the making of direct relationships between symbols and referents.[52] Such a mistaken, direct, relationship would as-

[50] *Ibid.*, pp. 10–12.   [51] *Ibid.*, p. 12.   [52] *Ibid.*, p. 2.

sume that the communicated content of a symbol is the same, or nearly the same, as the content of the thing it stands for, which is not usually or necessarily so.[53] It is easy to see a wide range of opportunity for ambiguity and inadequate definition in the atmosphere of such an assumption. But with this assumption denied, a word can mean many things to many people, can even mean different things to the same person at different times. It becomes necessary to check back to the referent if one is to understand the symbol. When a communicator uses a word he has so checked against the thing it stands for, he is much more likely to be clearly understood. It is for this reason that Richards so deplores any absolute doctrine of proper meaning[54] which assumes a direct, stable, and real relation between word and thing. Such a doctrine fails to take into account that the word stands for a host of different contexts, patterns, and associations for a different person or at a different time. If the reference is the pivot of the relation between symbol and referent, and if this pivotal reference is continually changing, enlarging, and enriching its contexts,[55] it is no wonder that the meaning of a symbol also undergoes change.

The psychological context of this pivotal reference is important, too. It explains the variability and ever-expanding breadth of the reference that goes with the symbol. For one word or symbol there can be as many references or thoughts as there are persons to think them. The communicator faces as many interpretations of his symbols as he has hearers, and even each of these is momentarily changing.[56] The hearer may be sure, when he hears a symbol, that it can mean something at least slightly dif-

[53] *Ibid.*, pp. 12 and 14–15.

[54] Richards, *The Philosophy of Rhetoric*, p. 11.

[55] Evidently, contexts must continually change, since fresh stimuli and responses are constantly being added to them as consciously remembered experience.

[56] The "protocol" experiments, to be explained later in this chapter, and embodied in *Practical Criticism* and *Interpretation in Teaching*, will illustrate the varieties of interpretation.

ferent from any meaning it may have had at any other time in his hearing.

The contextual theory of signs clearly allows inferences that could be formulated as rules or laws, the obeying of which might prevent mistakes of comprehension. Richards does draw these inferences and does formulate six laws, which he calls the "Canons of Symbolism."[57] They simply state Richards' logic in the form of precepts, as based upon the principles of contradiction and identity.

THE THEORY OF DEFINITION

The concept of defining here proposed owes its simplicity and directness to the fact that its groundwork has just been laid in the immediately preceding theory of thought–word–thing relationships.

Richards begins by clearing away what he calls "the barren subtleties of Genus and Differentia"[58] in the traditional theory of definition. For him, they lead to four difficulties which a practical theory must avoid:

1. Confusion between real and merely verbal definition, the defining of words and of things.

2. Confusion of symbol and referent in casual conversation; that is, "saying '*chien* means "dog" ' when we ought to say 'the word *chien* and the word "dog" both mean the same animal.' "

3. Forgetting that definitions are essentially "*ad hoc*"; in other words, "relevant to some purpose or situation and consequently are applicable only over a restricted field or 'universe of discourse.' " . . . "Whenever a term is thus taken outside the universe of discourse for which it has been defined, it becomes a metaphor, and may be in need of fresh definition."

4. Confusing intensive with extensive definitions. Accord-

---

[57] Ogden and Richards, *op. cit.*, pp. 87–108.   [58] *Ibid.*, p. 109.

ing to Richards an intensive definition calls for no change in the sign situation that is common to the person defining (or his reference) and the thing defined. No change is required because the definer prefers to stick to this one sign situation and analyze it alone and more intensively. In the case of the extensive definition, the definer seeks outside this sign situation and its context so as to compare it with other signs and contexts and to distinguish it clearly.[59]

Richards' answer to these four problems is the principle of indirect relationship between the symbol and the referent. Whenever there is a difficulty about what a symbol means, when there is a question of definition, look for the referent.[60] A referent common to all concerned, in a discussion for instance, must be found. If agreement cannot be reached this way, then other referents must be found upon which there is agreement, and from these the required referent can be evolved through its connections with the other referents.[61] These relations between the referents known and the referents to be found are classified by Richards under ten heads that seem to define very well the range of the communicator's interest:

1. Symbolization
2. Similarity
3. Spatial relations
4. Temporal relations
5. Causal relations of the physical kinds
6. Causal relations of the psychological kinds
7. Causal relations of the psychophysical kinds
8. Referent-reference relations (being the object of a mental state)
9. Common complex relations
10. Legal relations[62]

Clearly, one of the ways to find the referent for the term "cold war" would be to look for the well-known referents of the term

---

[59] *Ibid.*, pp. 111–112.
[61] *Ibid.*

[60] *Ibid.*, p. 113.
[62] *Ibid.*, pp. 114–120.

"cold" and "war." Then, by Richards' similarity relation, a new symbol, "a kind of war with no firing," is found. And this, after all, is really a beginning definition of "cold war" which was found by seeking the known referents behind the unknown one.

Richards then proceeds to describe the range of definition. He regrets that this range is sometimes falsely limited because of the persistent tendency to think of words as having proper and unalterable meanings.[63] He explains how kinds of defining may grow out of purposes in their immediate use. A definition for speculative discussion may be quite different from a definition of the same referent with a view to a practical operation. The subterfuges, by which speakers and writers sometimes suggest unchangeable definition where there really is no such thing, are listed by Richards. The phonetic subterfuge groups a hazy or emotive word, like "discrimination," with others similar in sound but clear in meaning like "dirt" and "death."[64] The hypostatic subterfuge uses the most overloaded and confusing universal or abstract terms, like "liberty" and "glory."[65] The utraquistic subterfuge uses words that have two meanings, such as the functional meaning of "knowledge" (knowing something), and the objective meaning (what is known).[66]

Up to this point Richards has been involved in highly speculative inquiry. While he has offered several practical rules of thumb, they were guides to efficient mental processes behind our rhetoric and communication rather than guides for immediate use in communicating.[67] At this point, however, he can take all this philosophy of rhetoric and apply it to what he feels is the most important single concern in an improved rhetoric or communication. He proposes that what needs thorough analysis, what needs to be adapted and applied to our symbol-using situation today,

[63] *Ibid.*, p. 123.
[64] *Ibid.*, pp. 133–134.
[65] *Ibid.*, p. 133.
[66] *Ibid.*, p. 134.
[67] Richards, *The Philosophy of Rhetoric*, p. 23.

is comprehension, efficient interpretation.[68] Consequently, all his speculative inquiries culminate in his still speculative, but nonethe less practical, instruments of comprehending.

TOWARD A THEORY OF COMPREHENDING

Although the clearest and most recent formulation of Richards' theory of comprehending is expressed in his latest book, *Speculative Instruments* (1955), the special research technique he uses to compile evidence for the theory is available only in *Practical Criticism* (1929) and *Interpretation in Teaching* (1938).

Faced with the emotive as well as the strictly referential content of language, Richards worked out a system which enabled him to give his students exercises in practical problems of interpretation and to gather evidence from these exercises about the roots of misunderstanding. The students, presented with identified passages of poetry and prose, voluntarily wrote protocols, or interpretations of the passages.[69] Richards' examination of these protocols revealed common patterns of frequently recurring kinds of mistakes, misinterpretations, meaning blocks, prejudices, preconceptions, and stock responses. From this information Richards developed a list of the ten difficulties readers generally have with poetry, and which also apply to prose:

1. Making out the plain sense
2. Sensuous apprehension
3. Imagery visualizing
4. Mnemonic irrelevances
5. Stock responses
6. Sentimentality
7. Inhibition
8. Doctrinal adhesions

[68] *Ibid.*, p. 3.   [69] Richards, *Practical Criticism*, pp. 3–4.

9. Technical presuppositions
10. General critical preconceptions.[70]

Such is the material used to substantiate Richards' contentions with regard to the dangerously slippery subject of emotion and value.[71]

It was with these experimental findings that he approached the most recent form of his theory of comprehending. We will need to summarize what Richards intends by the terms "comprehending," "meaning," and "interpreting." A comprehending is, of course, an accurate and true understanding, but is described by Richards as the nexus or context, or the network of contexts, that connect a whole series of past occurrences of partially similar utterances in partially similar situations.[72] This comprehension is the seizing of a meaning. It is the birth in the comprehending organism of a reference or a feeling or a tendency or a purpose. The meaning itself, which is seized, is first described by Richards as "the missing parts of its context."[73] He means, of course, the missing parts of the psychological and external contexts referred to in his contextual theory of signs. He means the reference with its contexts. Interpretation is the process of seizing this meaning and having this comprehension.

By "instruments," in *Speculative Instruments,* Richards means the norms used to compare alternative meanings so as to arrive at accurate and true comprehension. These instruments are the elements common to all utterances and also the elements about which questions must be asked by the interpreter, lest he run the risk of misunderstanding the utterance. It is these instru-

[70] *Ibid.,* pp. 12–15.

[71] Richards, *Interpretation in Teaching,* pp. 23–25.

[72] Richards, *Speculative Instruments* (Chicago: University of Chicago Press, 1955), pp. 23–24.

[73] Richards, *The Philosophy of Rhetoric,* p. 37.

ments that Richards hopes will be at the center of the organization of a new rhetoric.[74] He was aiming at these instruments all along through what, in earlier stages, he called "tasks of rhetoric," "aims of discourse," "language function," and "kinds of meaning."[75]

The seven instruments in question are listed here with Richards' own diagram to show that, even though they are interdependent, purpose has a special place in any instance of comprehending.[76]

1. Indicating
2. Characterizing
3. Realizing
4. Valuing
5. Influencing
6. Controlling
7. Purposing

Figure 2—From *Speculative Instruments*, by I. A. Richards
(University of Chicago Press, 1955), p. 26.
Used by permission.

He labels this diagram "Comprehending," since these are the sorts of work the communication utterance does to make itself comprehensible. They are the functions of the message working to be understood, as well as the functions of the interpreting mind trying to understand.[77]

[74] If, as we have seen, the theory of comprehension is the heart of Richards' new rhetoric, then his instruments of comprehending must also be central to it. See *Speculative Instruments*, p. 18, and *The Philosophy of Rhetoric*, p. 3.

[75] Richards, *Interpretation in Teaching*, pp. 12 and 15; *Principles of Literary Criticism*, p. 2; and *Practical Criticism*, pp. 75–76.

[76] Richards, *Speculative Instruments*, pp. 21 and 26.

[77] *Ibid.*, pp. 26–27.

Indicating is simply pointing out the referent of the symbol situation. *Characterizing* goes further. It says something about the referent (or thing); sorts it out, to some extent, from other things; attaches characteristics to it; finds a context for it that has been put together by a nexus of other contexts of previously experienced, similar situations. In the utterance to be comprehended, indicating and characterizing merely point out and segregate the referent.[78]

Realizing is not meant in the allowable sense of accomplishing something or bringing something to fruition, but in the sense of understanding, "having before the mind more fully, more consciously, more vividly than on occasions of less realization."[79] It can overlap with characterizing, but it does not need to do so. In fact, as Richards says: "All my seven components can vary independently, though they usually don't."[80]

Valuing is the assessing of the utterance from the vantage point of worth, obligation, or justice. But the assessing must be as philosophically neutral as it can be without losing its truly evaluative function. To exercise this valuing properly, according to Richards' plan, the interpreter need not—and, of course, in this connection, cannot—be detached. But he must be as neutral as possible.[81]

Influencing marks the state of wanting to "change or preserve unchanged"[82] whatever the utterance in question concerns. It is the throwing of the interpreter's weight to the side of keeping the uttered situation as it is or changing it.

Controlling or administering is the instrument that measures interpretations inasmuch as they are making the decisions of stability or change mentioned in the paragraph on influencing.

[78] *Ibid.*, pp. 28–31.
[79] From Richards' notes commenting on the first draft of the present study, Boston, December 7, 1956.
[80] *Ibid.*
[81] Richards, *Speculative Instruments*, pp. 34–35.
[82] *Ibid.*, p. 35.

Here the claims of the other instruments of the utterance are objectively balanced and organized by the interpreting mind.[83]

Purposing is the measuring of the intention, the motive, the end, of the utterance. Richards puts this instrument in the central position in the diagram, not because purpose has a higher importance in any hierarchical sense, but because purpose is connected with that original drive of the organism to express itself. The purpose of the utterance is connected with that twofold cause of the use of language in all situations: the inner needs of the organism and the stimulations it receives from outside.[84]

While the first two of these instruments are usually primary, there is no need that they be so. The measuring and comparing that go on in each succeeding application of the seven instruments to the comprehending situation will be modified by the applications of the instruments that have been applied to it earlier.[85] Thus characterizing may be fuller and more detailed because it happens after realizing than if it were to happen before realizing. The seven instruments have no special order of application, no distinct sequence, no separation necessarily in time. But "they are all of them coactive together inextricably all the time."[86]

There is no necessary or set hierarchy in the interrelationships of these new instruments:

> There is thus at the heart of any theory of meaning a principle of the instrument. The exploration of comprehension is the task of devising a system of instruments for comparing meanings. But these systems, these instruments, are themselves comparable. They belong with what they compare and are subject in the end to one another. Indeed this mutual subjection and control seems to be the ἀρχή for a doctrine of comprehension—that upon which all else depends.[87]

Thus the mutual control these instruments exercise over one another is the ἀρχή or first principle of the theory. The instruments

---

[83] *Ibid.*, pp. 36–38.   [84] *Ibid.*, pp. 19–22.   [85] *Ibid.*, pp. 27–28.

[86] From Richards' notes commenting on the first draft of the present study, Boston, December 7, 1956.

[87] Richards, *Speculative Instruments*, pp. 18–19.

are the yardsticks or calipers according to which the comparisons of meanings are to be made.[88] Nor does this system of instruments concern only the reader–hearer end of the communication unit. The writer–speaker can use these instruments too, to purify, clarify, and objectivize his communication.[89] But most important of all is the consideration that the education of efficient comprehenders amounts to the preparation of efficiently comprehending audiences which, presumably, would not long put up with the pervading and flagrant ambiguities and distortions of meaning to be found in so much of current spoken and printed material. Presumably, also, an exacting demand would be created for the type of communicator who has been educated to this kind of efficient comprehension, and has become accustomed to subjecting his utterances to a like efficient scrutiny with similar normative principles and instruments.[90] He would, in other words, be behaving as his own first audience to pretest the offering of his own communication.

The sense of these seven instruments and their applicability becomes much clearer when Richards translates them into questions the interpreter may ask himself about different comparable interpretations he may see in any utterances. These questions correspond in number and order to the instruments themselves. Referring to such comparable interpretations, he asks:

1. How far do they pick out the same (or at least analogous) things to talk about?
2. How far do they say the same (or at least analogous) things about them?
3. How far do they present with equal vividness and/or actuality, weak or strong?
4. How far do they value in the same ways?

[88] *Ibid.*, pp. 19 and 26.
[89] Clearly, both the instruments and the parallel questions Richards derives from them (pages 52 and 53) are as workable for the communicator preparing his communication as for the interpreter comprehending a communication.
[90] Richards, *The Philosophy of Rhetoric*, pp. 3, 8–11, 23–24, and 37.

5. How far would they keep or change in the same ways?
6. How far are the dependencies and interplay between 1, 2, 3, 4, 5, and 6 itself the same in them both?
7. How widely would they serve the same purposes, playing the same parts, within the varying activities they might occur in?[91]

Richards also goes about the business of connecting his instruments with the sociology and psychology of communication. Taking the Shannon and Weaver diagram[92] of communication and making some small changes to suit his purposes better, he first inserts the fields of comparison[93] so that the relation can be seen between the operation of the principles of communication and the operating fields of the instruments (Fig. 3). Then, turn-

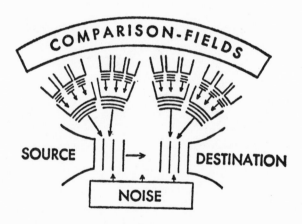

Figure 3—From *Speculative Instruments,* by I. A. Richards (University of Chicago Press, 1955), p. 23. Used by permission.

[91] Richards, *Speculative Instruments,* p. 27.
[92] Claude E. Shannon and Warren Weaver, *The Mathematical Theory of Communication* (Urbana, Ill.: University of Illinois Press, 1949), p. 5.
[93] Richards, *Speculative Instruments,* p. 23.

ing the diagram out ninety degrees and looking down it as one might aim down the length of a pole, he shows the relational position of the instruments themselves (Fig. 4). The instrument diagram has now been fitted on to the pole of the communication diagram, much like a wheel upon an axle. The fields of comparison in Figure 3 are, of course, represented as containing many different and comparable readings or meanings or interpretations of the communicated utterance. Consequently they are comparison fields in the sense that it is here that the interpreting mind will be making its measurings and sortings according to the seven instruments on the wheel that encircles the fields at an angle of ninety degrees in Figure 4.[94]

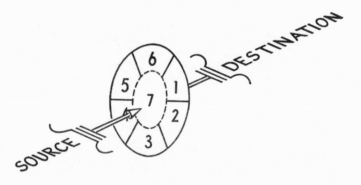

FIGURE 4

These instruments as components of his system of comprehension are the heart and the head of Richards' proposed new rhetoric, the core of a discipline that will take the place of the old rhetoric among the liberal arts.[95] A grasp of such things and much practice and exercising in them is Richards' tentative answer to the rhetoric problem. As we saw in the early pages of this

[94] *Ibid.*, pp. 25–26.   [95] Richards, *The Philosophy of Rhetoric*, p. 3.

analysis of Richards' theory, he is dissatisfied with the way current rhetoric concentrates upon the mere devices of persuasive composition and speech. He wants a whole treatment of man's symbol-using power in prose, its philosophy as well as its practical application. He proposes that this wholeness should be reflected in a new teaching rhetoric for classroom use.[96]

[96] *Ibid.*, p. 9.

CHAPTER 3

Kenneth Burke's Theory

To UNDERSTAND THE RHETORIC THEORY OF KENNETH BURKE, IT is essential to point to its roots in sociology and psychology. According to Burke, man pours all his energies into establishing and maintaining his personal world of hierarchic order. His survival depends on it. And rhetoric is his specific means of seeking or keeping that order. Not only in intrapersonal relations, where man uses his rhetoric on himself, where he holds inner parliament as both speaker and hearer, but, in all his interpersonal, intergroup, and interclass relations, he is striving for status in an accepted order, for survival by social balance with his inner self and with his world.[1] Rhetoric, then, is the instrument of strife, because it is the means of defending and competing for this order. But it is also the means of accomplishing order, because, for Burke, entreaty, overture, politeness, and diplomacy are all forms of a rhetoric of courtship that promotes union for the sake of order:

[1] Kenneth Burke, *A Rhetoric of Motives* (New York: George Braziller, Inc., c1950), p. 39.

The *Rhetoric* must lead us through the Scramble, the Wrangle of the Market Place, the flurries and flare-ups of the Human Barnyard, the Give and Take . . . .[2]

Yet, on the other hand:

Rhetoric also includes resources of appeal . . . .[3]

It too has its peaceful moments: at times its endless competition can add up to the transcending of itself. In ways of its own, it can move from factional to universal.[4]

Out of the frequent and lengthy conversations between Burke and the present writer,[5] this rhetoric of peace and union emerges as a kind of central theme. He seems to have dedicated his work to the fashioning of peace. His theory of rhetoric pervades all his work. It is directed toward the achievement of peace, as the highest end for which he could have been born.

Burke differs from Aristotle and Richards in some ways. His work is an extension of Aristotelian rhetoric rather than a conflicting theory.[6] The extension, however, is so vast, both in the new broadness of his concept of rhetoric and in its applicability to modern life, that he calls it a "new"[7] rhetoric. Beyond the evident difference between the psychobiological approach of Richards and the sociopsychological approach of Burke, the essential points of comparison between them might be found by contrasting Richards' central interest in a scientific method of interpretation with Burke's preoccupation with dramatistic motiva-

[2] *Ibid.*, p. 23. Reprinted with permission of Prentice-Hall, Inc., from *A Rhetoric of Motives* by Kenneth Burke; copyright, 1950, by Prentice-Hall, Inc.
[3] *Ibid.*, p. 19. [4] *Ibid.*, p. 23.
[5] Mr. Burke was kind enough to take an enthusiastic interest in this chapter, giving his time frequently and at great length to explain his position, and to read and comment extensively upon a first outline and two subsequent drafts. Interviews and letters as well as his lengthy notes on this summary of his theory will be quoted from time to time.
[6] Burke, *A Rhetoric of Motives*, Introduction, p. x.
[7] Kenneth Burke, "Rhetoric Old and New," *The Journal of General Education*, V (April, 1951), p. 203.

tion.[8] While Burke was interested enough in interpretation to give that name to the first published version of the opening section of *Permanence and Change* (1935)[9] he was much more interested in attitude than in comprehension. At the same time, even though Richards' studies lean more toward the scientific aspects of meaning than toward motivational meaning, still motive is at the heart of his instruments of interpretation. Many additional points of comparison will occur to the reader in the subsequent study of Burke's philosophy of rhetoric. But explicit attention to them will be reserved for Chapter 5, where all three emergent theories will be extended to proposals for a modern teaching rhetoric.

We turn now to the six aspects of Burke's rhetoric: his background and approach to rhetoric; his pentad format; his theory of abstraction and the negative; his theory of definition and identification; his philosophy of literary form; and the instrumental applications of his theory.

THE BACKGROUND AND APPROACH TO RHETORIC

For many younger scholars and teachers in composition and communication courses, *The Philosophy of Literary Form* (1941) provided a first acquaintance with Burke's ideas. But there was already a substantial bibliography, beginning with *Counter-Statement* (1931, revised in 1953), *Permanence and Change* (1935, revised in 1954), and *Attitudes Toward History* (1937). His interest in the psychology and sociology of motivation grew as he edited publications for the Bureau of Social Hygiene and made sustained contributions to *The Dial, The Nation,* and *The Republic.* In the meantime he lectured on literary criticism at the University of Chicago in 1938 and again in 1949, and at

* From Burke's comments on the first draft of this summary, Andover, New Jersey, December 22, 1956.
* *Ibid.*

Bennington College since 1939. Publications and lectures alike showed a man obviously at home in the fields of sociology, psychology, philosophy, and linguistics. Since the appearance of *The Philosophy of Literary Form* (1941), Burke has published two volumes of a planned four-volume series on the language of motivation. *A Grammar of Motives* (1945) discusses the grammatical–logical dimension of language, and *A Rhetoric of Motives* (1950) explains the rhetorical dimension. The two volumes yet unpublished, *A Symbolic of Motives* and *On Human Relations,* will treat the poetic and ethical dimensions of language respectively.[10]

The troubled socioeconomic environment of Burke's maturing years had as much influence upon his later theory as the books he was reading at that time. Life in New York City during the Great Depression and the social and psychological phenomena to be observed there during two world wars were as much a part of his young manhood as Aristotle, Kant, Bentham, and Veblen.[11] Through the economic, social, and ideological strife of those years he was reading Bergson on the negative and de Gourmont on dissociation. "In fact," he says, "Remy de Gourmont was almost a 'traumatic' experience in my development."[12] Both from conversational reassurances to the writer and the opening remarks of "Curriculum Criticum"[13] in *Counter-Statement,* it is evident that the industrial–cultural conflicts of a large city were somewhat similarly traumatic for him. As soon as he was able to do so, he left New York and sought geographic and intellectual peace in a relatively untouched part of New Jersey.

All these readings and experiences led Burke to make an essential connection between language and the nature of man.

[10] Kenneth Burke, *Counter-Statement* (2nd ed. rev.; Los Altos, Calif.: Hermes Publications, 1953), pp. 217–218.

[11] Interview with Kenneth Burke, Andover, New Jersey, January 3, 1957.

[12] From Burke's comments on the first draft of this summary, Andover, New Jersey, December 22, 1956.

[13] Burke, *Counter-Statement,* pp. 213–214.

Man is not just a rational animal. He is a "symbol-using animal,"[14] because his use of symbols is what makes him specifically different from other animals. Also, it is in the use of symbols that a man differentiates himself from other men as he puts his personally projected world in the kind of order he can live with. Further, it is through symbols that he relates himself with others so that, in his organized system of interdependency, he may satisfy his needs. The simplest visceral urgency within him, he translates, with the help of his symbol-making power, into a gesture or phrase that modifies the visceral urgency, or explains it away, but always in terms of the order he is building for himself. For Burke, the whole range of this activity, from a man's inner, subconscious conflicts to the highest kind of conscious abstraction, is rhetoric.[15]

Realizing that this human search for internal and external order provided the motivation for the exercise of rhetoric, Burke began to look for some method or pattern of inquiry with which to discern the meaningful motives behind rhetorical language.

THE PENTAD FORMAT

At some time during the preparation of *A Grammar of Motives,* Burke devised what he calls his pentad format. It served him as a method of inquiry; but it also developed, as we shall see, into a practical instrument for the application of his theory to a teaching rhetoric. There were developmental stages before the mature format evolved. It seems to have begun with a dialectical, many-angled examination of a problem. Inside his own thinking process, he would state his case, refute his statement, and then formulate a compromise or a neutral, residual statement.[16] Later, realizing that this gave him only two viewpoints at most, he began to exercise his aptitudes for etymological analysis, and ac-

[14] Letter from Kenneth Burke, Andover, New Jersey, September 20, 1956.
[15] Burke, *A Rhetoric of Motives,* p. 41.
[16] Interview with Kenneth Burke, Andover, New Jersey, January 3, 1957.

quired at least another dimension for the same problem. He justifies this kind of dialectical horseplay by asking:

Is not the intention always to keep oneself reminded of the linguistic element that necessarily interposes itself between the symbol-using animal and the nonsymbolic reality?[17]

And further on in the same context, realizing that puns are in the same etymological class of split meanings, he says:

Puns involve a sensory element, but are certainly not confined to this, particularly the abstruse kinds that seem to figure in metaphysics, or in theological analogies such as word-Word.[18]

Thus the varieties of senses gathered from etymological roots and accepted usages of terms provide Burke with the multiple aspects he can use to examine a problem.

The next step is from the dialectical to the symposium type of inner personal discussion. It is as though Burke were a five- or six-man discussion group, taking all the speaking parts himself until he has sifted the best resultant formulation of the idea in question. All this seems necessary to Burke, even in his thinking, because, early in his career, he convinced himself that any one statement or point of view was necessarily only a part of the attainable truth. It was a kind of part statement, a synecdochic half-meaning at best. So he resolved to keep going back and looking again from a different point of view, until the common, consistent, undeniable meaning stood out unmistakably. Describing this symposium kind of dialectic, Burke says:

Ideally, all the various "voices" are partisan rhetoricians whose partial voices "competitively cooperate" to form the position of the dialogue as a whole (a position that transcends all the partial views of the participants, though there may be a Socratic voice that is *primus inter pares*).[19]

---

[17] From Burke's comments on the first draft of this summary, Andover, New Jersey, December 22, 1956.
[18] *Ibid.*   [19] *Ibid.*

Finally, however, still questing for the best organized method of making repeated beginnings, he saw that the principles or bases from which the repeated starts were to be made must be so fundamental that they would apply to any problem or topic to be looked at.[20] It was at this point that he hit upon what he calls his "pentad" of aspects. This involves what Burke feels is a fivefold viewpoint of anything whatever that a man can discuss. For any action (human, symbol-using act), as opposed to motion (mere animal, nonsymbol-using act), there are always these five points of view: *scene,* the environmental point of view; *act,* the thing itself as represented in an idea; *agent,* the derivational or efficient cause aspect of the thing; *agency,* the "how" and "with what assistance"[21] of the thing or act; and *purpose,* the agent's motivation. Burke now has five questions to ask about any topic or problem, five ways to express fullness of meaning, five ways for the receiver of the communication to test it for deeper motivational meaning behind the symbols. He can not only repeatedly begin his examination, but he can know he is asking the basic and most important and exhaustive questions each time he returns to begin again. In fact, by permutations of pairs of the five questions, he really has ten questions to ask, ten points from which to repeat a beginning: act–scene, act–agent, act–agency, act–purpose, scene–agent, scene–agency, scene–purpose, agent–agency, agent–purpose, and agency–purpose.[22] These are the bases of the repeated-beginnings method of Burke. This, with its terms culled from critical analysis of the drama, is what he calls his dramatistic[23] approach to language and to rhetoric. A term, then, or a symbol, and with it its idea and its referent too, must be looked at much in the same manner as a unit of dramatic action upon a stage. To be understood it must be viewed as an *act,* as the act of *whom,* as *how,* as *where,* and as *why.* The in-

[20] Kenneth Burke, *A Grammar of Motives* (copyright, 1945, by Prentice-Hall, Inc., Englewood Cliffs, N.J.), Introduction, p. xvi.

[21] *Ibid.,* pp. xv–xvii. [22] *Ibid.,* pp. xix–xxi. [23] *Ibid.,* p. xxii.

teresting similarity between these pentad forms and the "four ultimate causes" of Aristotle only reassured Burke of their basic nature.[24] The similarity with the alternate questions that Scholastic philosophers asked themselves is also striking: *Quis? Quid? Quibus auxiliis? Ubi? Cur? Quomodo? Quando?* (Who? What? With what assistance? Where? Why? How? When?).[25] The fundamental rule of thumb that used to be taught to journalism students as a way of covering all the pertinent details of a news event indicates how functionally useful is this metaphysical classification.[26] Sociological research, also, has provided a communication model based on studies in control, content, audience, situation, and effect—really extensions in application of the Lasswell "formula."[27]

With this method of inquiry Burke expects to be able to ferret out the motivational meaning of symbols and symbol clusters that we all use in the organization and protection of the order we need for survival. A second perusal of Burke's important books and writings, based upon a thorough understanding of this method, can prove rewarding. It might also be helpful to the reader who is searching for familiar order in Burke's writings. The train of thought is really dialectical. While his works are not explicit dialogues, he admits that he often thinks and writes in dialogue—or better still, in "pantalogue"—form to embrace all possible facets of any topic under discussion.[28]

Although the pentad format began as a methodology, and

[24] Interview with Kenneth Burke, Andover, New Jersey, January 3, 1957, confirmed this basic similarity. See Aristotle, "Metaphysica," in *The Basic Works of Aristotle*, ed. Richard McKeon, trans. Rhys Roberts *et al.* (New York: Random House, Inc., 1941; originally published by Oxford University Press in 1928), i, ii, and iii, pp. 689–731 (980a–1003a).

[25] Burke, *Counter-Statement* p. 141.

[26] George F. Mott *et al., An Outline Survey of Journalism* (rev. ed.; New York: Barnes and Noble, Inc., 1943), pp. 62–63.

[27] Lyman Bryson, ed., *The Communication of Ideas* (New York: Harper & Brothers, 1948), pp. 37–38.

[28] Interview with Kenneth Burke, Andover, New Jersey, January 3, 1957.

proved itself, soon after, as an efficient instrument in the discernment of motivation,[29] its further use as a format for the practice of Burke's rhetoric of peace and union does not become clear until it is considered in connection with the projections and extensions of a modern discussion rhetoric in Chapter 5.

We can now turn to the several aspects of Burke's philosophy of rhetoric: abstraction and the negative; definition and identification; and philosophy of literary form.

THE THEORY OF ABSTRACTION AND THE NEGATIVE

Abstraction and the negative are so intimately related in Burke's philosophy that clarity is the only possible excuse for the separate treatment they are given here.

THEORY OF ABSTRACTION

Abstraction is, for Burke, almost everything it was for Aristotle. The rational mind's power to separate and classify and collect on a choice basis is part of Burke's theory of abstraction, though he has not always come to it by the same route nor in the same terminology.[30] Furthermore, even the word–thought–thing relationships, which are of course basic to abstraction, are realist in the epistemological theory of Burke. The thought is real with that metaphysical reality that realists give to ideas that represent real things conceptually.[31]

With such an introduction, Burke can be considered as having two things to say about abstraction. First, it is the characteristically human ability that makes a rational man specifically rational. Not only is this abstracting power, which Burke calls

---

[29] From Burke's notes commenting on the first draft of this summary, Andover, New Jersey, December 22, 1956.

[30] Kenneth Burke, "A Dramatistic View of the Origins of Language," Part I, *The Quarterly Journal of Speech*, XXXVIII (October, 1952), pp. 256–259.

[31] *Ibid.*, p. 259.

"generalization," the specific element of his essence as a man, but it lifts his nature, in kind as well as in degree, above that of other animals. Burke arrives at this conclusion by comparing the non-conceptual sorting and selecting that animals experience with the rational kind of abstracting or generalizing. This is how he sums up:

> When we call attention to the rudiments of generalization, specifica-tion, classification, and abstraction in the conditioning and adapta-tions of non-linguistic organisms, we do not mean to derive 'rational' human language by a simple 'graded series' from the 'behavioristic pre-language' of sensation and gesture. On the contrary, we subscribe to the view that there is a 'qualitative leap' between the motives of pre-language and those of language. . . .
> Hence to say that the principles of abstraction, classification, gen-eralization, and specification (or division) are present in pre-linguistic behavior is not the same as saying that their linguistic analogues are 'nothing but' more complicated variants of the pre-linguistic.[32]

ON THE NEGATIVE

The second thing Burke has to say about abstraction con-nects with his theory of the negative and illustrates what he calls the highest kind of symbol-using activity of which man is capable, symbol-using about symbols themselves (as opposed to symbol-using about things), the conscious use of words to talk about words. The theory of the negative comes up here because it is his way of pointing out man's essential difference from nonabstract-ing animals. If the abstracting process could be shown to be es-sentially different from the elemental animal sorting, then the essential difference of kind between man and other animals would be clear. Burke considered the Empiricists' theory of ideas. Their approach to the whole idea problem was to reduce the idea to an image and thus materialize it. With every idea reducible to the material, there would be no need to postulate any special kind of metaphysical reality for ideas at all.[33] Burke proposed, on the

---

[32] *Ibid.*, p. 257.   [33] *Ibid.*, pp. 259–260.

other hand, an idea that cannot be so reduced to image and thus materialized. That idea was the idea of *no* or *not*, or, in other words, the negative.[34] It is Burke's contention that *not* can be conceived, in an idea, and yet one can have no image of it. All the images one has in connection with it are not really its image but images of the real things of which it is the negation. As he says,

Though idea and image have become merged in the development of language, the negative provides the instrument for splitting them apart. *For the negative is an idea;* there can be no image of it. *But in imagery there is no negative.*[35]

The negative, then, is the sole example of an idea that cannot be empirically reduced to material. In the capacity to symbolize this negative lies the specific feature of man's linguistic function that is impossible to animals. Burke sums it up:

The essential distinction between the verbal and the nonverbal is in the fact that language adds the peculiar possibility of the negative.[36]

It is pertinent to note that it is in his theory of the negative that Burke traces the origins and development of language. With the most primitive operation of this negative in early language, men first began to show the ability to symbolize. "No's" and cautionary expletives and warnings and protests were not, even then, the mere *positive* turning away of the animal's mouth from what was unpleasant food, but a real head shaking.[37] The growth of the negative was, by and large, the evolution of language. He traces that evolution of the negative from the negative command to the positive attitude *not* to break that command, and on to the

[34] Burke took Bergson's "nothing," changed it to "not" and "no," and insisted upon the hortatory negative (thou shalt not) rather than the propositional negative (it is not) of Bergson. For Burke, it is here in the hortatory negative—"no" and "not"—that we can find the deepest root of language as specifically and essentially human in its symbol-using function. From an interview with Kenneth Burke, New York, May 29, 1957.

[35] Burke, "A Dramatistic View of the Origins of Language," p. 260.

[36] *Ibid.*, Part III, XXXIX (February, 1953), p. 79.

[37] *Ibid.*, Part I, XXXVIII (October, 1952), p. 257.

propositional or declarative negative.[38] And all the while his great objective is to show his readers that everything is imbued with the negative because it usually implies, at least when the selecting and generalizing are in operation, a limiting and shifting and sorting that, in themselves, mean continually saying no. Choosing will immediately imply saying no, at least to all the things one is ruling out when he is being selective, or exact, or even when he is being general and abstract, because he is classifying.[39]

The importance of this abstracting and of what it tends to make us include and exclude in our habitual symbolizing processes will become clearer as we move on to the study of definition and identification.

THE THEORY OF DEFINITION AND IDENTIFICATION

This section will deal with a definition theory and several ambiguities of defining and naming. Then it will introduce motivation in the Burkeian sense before proceeding to a discussion of identification and hierarchy.

DEFINITION

Burke has no specific quarrel with the classic theory of genus and species definition.[40] But he does concentrate on a more usable kind of defining that identifies not only genera and species, but individuals as well. It is a kind of defining that brings modern rhetoric very close to linguistics.

A sentence or proposition points out its subject very clearly, even in the definitional sense, if its order of words allows for a gradual transition from the abstract to the concrete. Burke's example will serve best to illustrate this: "This good man runs very swiftly."[41] Now, this statement makes a predication about a good

---

[38] *Ibid.*, pp. 252 and 262. [39] *Ibid.*, pp. 256–257.
[40] Burke, *A Grammar of Motives*, pp. 409–410.
[41] Burke, "A Dramatistic View of the Origins of Language," Part III, XXXIX (February, 1953), pp. 88–89.

man. It says he is one who runs swiftly. Burke explains that in the first three words, *this good man*, the idea man, which is as abstract as that reference can be made, is gradually delimited and narrowed down until the other kinds of men (not good) are all ruled out, and finally delimited again until every other man, good or not, except *this* one, is ruled out. The subject, then, has been exactly defined, pinpointed inescapably. Similarly, the general action in *runs* is delimited by its two modifiers, *swiftly* and *very*, until it is nearly as well defined. Then by combination with the substantive half of the sentence, even this action part of it comes to be more accurately defined, and so the whole sentence has its subject and his action exactly defined by this grammatical combination of functions, supplementing the order of words. The more abstract ideas, with which the process is begun, are the genera. The more accurate and concrete ideas, after the process of reduction, are the species and individuals that are defined.[42]

In addition to this double way of defining, illustrated in the one example above, namely by order of words and by grammatical function, Burke cites a third way: by growth of vocabulary. Growth of vocabulary refers to the use of more and more accurate words that pinpoint and demonstrate the subject or action.[43] Such pinpointing amounts to defining because it delimits and points at the object.

But in spite of a clear theory of definition, there is still great possibility of misdirection and inaccuracy in defining. Burke has singled out four general kinds of defining that are sources of ambiguity.

Contextual definition defines, not by describing the thing itself, but by relating it to some other thing in its context.[44] This is clearly not the same thing as the context definition implied in Richards' theory of context. Richards wants the richness of perti-

[42] *Ibid.*, pp. 88–92. [43] *Ibid.*, pp. 88–89.
[44] Burke, *A Grammar of Motives*, p. 24.

nent surroundings and connectives to help us see a Gestalt view of the thing to be defined. Burke wants to be sure we do not emphasize the context at the expense of the subject itself. To try to define a class of people by describing their environment without any description of the people would be giving their class a contextual definition in Burke's sense.[45] Definers who do this lay themselves open to the charge that they are failing to discuss the class of people in themselves.[46] Of course, this kind of defining is one extreme whose converse is just as faulty. To try to define a class without any reference to their contextual surroundings of environment would omit as much of the true sense as would contextual defining.

Derivational definition defines the thing by its sources. Sources, however, are often so highly abstract in a definitional statement that they allow many different meanings. Burke examines the terms *general, generic,* and *genitive* etymologically and finds ambiguity. He points out that, though all these three terms have a common etymological root pointing to familial derivation, they have vastly different meanings. According to *The American College Dictionary, general* means: "pertaining to, affecting, including, or participated in by all members of a class or group; not partial or particular."[47] According to the same source, *generic* seems to have the Peripatetic–Scholastic meaning as its first and most usual one, "pertaining to a genus." *Genitive,* still in the same source, carries the grammatical sense as its first meaning: "denoting the case of nouns generally used to modify other nouns, often indicating possession, but used also in expressions of measure, origin, characteristic."[48]

Circumference shifting refers to the tendency any one per-

[45] From Burke's notes commenting on the first draft of this summary, Andover, New Jersey, December 22, 1956.

[46] Burke, *A Grammar of Motives,* p. 26.

[47] *The American College Dictionary,* ed. Clarence L. Barnhart (New York: Random House, Inc., copyright 1947), p. 505.

[48] *Ibid.,* p. 506.

son may have to shift the area of context of his term, agreed upon at the start, to a slightly new context which now has much that it had before but has dropped off some of the context from one edge of the rim and picked up new elements on the other edge.

Now, it seems undeniable, by the very nature of the case, that in definition, or systematic placement, one must see things "in terms of . . ." And implicit in the terms chosen, there are "circumferences" of varying scope.[49]

If the totality of the context, for instance, of the term "street" were agreed upon by two discussants in Springfield, Illinois, they might both mean an average city street with a tree or two, some ordinary buildings, traffic, and so on. But if one of them is from Manhattan and the other from a village in Vermont, it will be understandable how the New Englander may soon slip off to where he has more shady trees and less traffic on his "street," and the Manhattanite may have begun to introduce a huge electric sign, or traffic jams, or increased noise. The two discussants would have moved away from one another and would soon have two different definitions for "street." They would, in effect, no longer be talking about the same thing.

The ambiguity source of *scope–reduction–deflection* is somewhat similar but refers to the relative sizes and directions of the circumference of an idea that two discussants might have.[50] As usual, Burke looks at it in terms of act, scene, and the like:

A given act is in effect a different act, *depending upon the scope of the scene in terms of which it is located, or defined.* Define the act in terms of a scene comprising a whole pantheon of warring deities, and it is of one sort; define it in terms of a single God, and it is another sort; define it in terms of godless "nature," and it is another sort; define it in such terms as "The West," or "Victorianism," or "capitalism," or "an apartment in Soho, July 12, 1887," and it is of

---

[49] Burke, *A Grammar of Motives*, p. 77.   [50] *Ibid.*, pp. 77–85.

correspondingly other sorts. Yet there is no set rule for such a choice of scope ("in terms of" which it is to be defined).[51]

The reduction factor is the sloughing off of some or any of the elements of the context so that the context becomes smaller or more concrete than it was when the discussions started, thus affording two different definitions and consequent ambiguity.[52] The factor of deflection in this ambiguity source entails reduction toward a smaller context that leaves out the pertinent elements upon which the discussion depends. The New Englander and the Manhattanite might get into this kind of difficulty if one of them began to talk about "street" as though its essential element were either the village hotel porch with its dozing octogenarians, or, perhaps, the newsstand near the subway entrance.

It is important to remember that, in Burke's thinking, the four kinds of definitional ambiguity just described are not only notable because their ambiguity makes for unclear communication and reception, but, even more especially, because they are the symbol-user's conscious or unconscious ways of getting away from the kind of meaning that does not fit his motivations.[53] It is part of the fortunate richness of language that makes it possible for people to adjust themselves to reality. Personally and subjectively, it allows them to be blind to reality in one spot and not in another. The great point about this kind of ambiguity, as about every kind of motivational manipulation of symbols, is that it must be understood thoroughly by those who wish to receive and communicate real meaning—motivational meaning.

Hence, instead of considering it our task to "dispose of" any ambiguity by merely disclosing the fact that it is an ambiguity, we rather consider it our task to study and clarify the *resources* of ambiguity.[54]

[51] From Burke's notes commenting on the first draft of this summary, Andover, New Jersey, December 22, 1956.
[52] Burke, *A Grammar of Motives*, p. 96.
[53] *Ibid.*, Introduction, p. xviii.   [54] *Ibid.*, p. xix.

Roots for a New Rhetoric

To point momentarily at where Burke hopes rhetoric of this kind will eventually lead, it is sufficient to visualize a group of discussants with subjective blind spots due to diverse motivations. They might, in a kind of dialectical give and take, light up one another's blind spots, fill out contexts, unify circumferences, and generally come to some residual and mutual agreement both in understanding and action.[55]

MOTIVATION

Motivation can now be explicitly described. It is the beginning, the continuity, and the end of Burke's theory of rhetoric. But it comes into special prominence as the explanation of definition and naming habits in symbol-using. Burke describes motivation as "shorthand terms for situations" and as "rough shorthand descriptions for certain typical patterns of discrepant and conflicting stimuli"[56] that pull us one way or the other and make us explain to ourselves and others why we went the way we did.

We are now free to deal with "pair terms" as motivational language subterfuges. Parenthetically it may be well to repeat that Burke is not considering these things as conscious dishonesties or unconscious dodges. He is interested in analyzing them neutrally to see the motivation behind them.

Accordingly, what we want is not *terms that avoid ambiguity*, but *terms that clearly reveal the strategic spots at which ambiguities arise.*[57]

He wants us to learn them and let them help us understand one another better in the interests of union, cooperation, and peace.

The "love–duty"[58] *pair term* will exemplify this meaning of

[55] From Burke's notes commenting on the first draft of this summary, Andover, New Jersey, December 22, 1956.
[56] Kenneth Burke, *Permanence and Change* (rev. ed.; Los Altos, Calif.: Hermes Publications, 1954), pp. 29–30.
[57] Burke, *A Grammar of Motives*, Introduction, p. xviii.
[58] See Burke, *op. cit.*, Chapters 4 and 5, for numerous examples of other pairwords that name accepted patterns of attitude and scene that we call motives.

72

motivation. The young clerk resists a temptation to throw up his job and elope because, as he feels or says, he is motivated by duty. "Duty" in this case could be the motivational term used, perhaps unconsciously, to conceal the rejection of something relatively pleasant (elopement) in favor of the long-view retention of something much more pleasant to him (security and respect). The term "duty" makes him appear to his whole social milieu, and possibly even to himself, as characterful, steady, dependable, and level-headed. But this pair term would also serve him well if his decision had been the exact opposite. For he could, after the elopement, consider himself, and perhaps be considered by others, as romantic, virile, courageous, honest, and forthright, because he put love above all else. It is clear that, for Burke, the love–duty pair is one of those basic, ambiguous, definitional, or naming situations that is vague enough to cover any adjustment to pleasant or unpleasant events. The further important point here is that this ambiguity is, in Burke's opinion, nothing to be bewailed or deplored.

I am merely attempting to suggest that a terminology of motives is not evasive or self-deceptive, but is moulded to fit our general orientation as to purposes, instrumentalities, the "good life," etc.[59]

It is wonderful that language permits such adjustments. It is only necessary that each one should, according to his lights and his opportunities, examine and bring to consciousness these hidden motivations, if he is to use rhetoric to avoid disturbed communication and establish a workable basis for human action and cooperation.[60]

Other pair terms like "piety–impiety"[61] and "the sacrifice and the kill"[62] illustrate ambiguity of motivation and of terms in a similar fashion. Often, too, the symbol-user will build what Burke

[59] Burke, *Permanence and Change*, p. 29.
[60] *Ibid.*, pp. 23–25.   [61] *Ibid.*, pp. 74–88.
[62] Kenneth Burke, *The Philosophy of Literary Form* (Baton Rouge, La.: Louisiana State University Press, 1941), pp. 46–51.

calls "eulogistic and dyslogistic"[63] labels for his acts, that enable him to indulge, whether consciously or not, for himself or for others, in limitless motivational window dressing. Depending on one's known or unknown motive or situation, he can describe industry either as "planned economy" or as "regimentation." Care with details can be labeled "fussiness" or "painstaking method."

IDENTIFICATION

All this theory of definition and motivational naming brings us, at last, to the central element of Burke's rhetoric theory. That central element is "identification,"[64] the central concept in his whole motivation theory.

Burke does not intend, by "identification," the meaning so often associated with personal identification or identification cards. Nor does he mean the metaphysical notion of identification which calls for an absolute oneness of identity. That would call identical what was once mistakenly thought to be two similar objects and is later found to be one and the same object. One could lose his hat, see what looked like another and think how similar the two hats look, only to find that the one he now sees is really the same, identical hat that he lost. Burke's identification is really consubstantiality. It means that things or people, different in other ways, may have one common factor in which they are consubstantial or substantially the same.

A doctrine of *consubstantiality*, either explicit or implicit, may be necessary to any way of life. For substance, in the old philosophies, was an *act*; and a way of life is an *acting-together*; and in acting together, men have common sensations, concepts, images, ideas, attitudes that make them *consubstantial*.[65]

Thus members of the Elks Club have identity in their common interest in the Elks. They acquire identification with all the other members under this common factor of membership. In this

[63] Burke, *A Rhetoric of Motives*, pp. 90–101.
[64] *Ibid.*, pp. 19–23.   [65] *Ibid.*, p. 21.

Burkeian sense, people identify themselves with causes, religions, movements, with heroic types in the movies, with classes or types of people who buy any given make of motorcar or live in one or another neighborhood. Identification, then, is a belonging to a group of people or a becoming one with them through at least some one formality of common purpose or ideal.[66] As applied to rhetoric in this sense, identification says everything that persuasion says, since it is by becoming one with readers or hearers, in this way, that the rhetorician attempts to persuade.

As for the relation between "identification" and "persuasion": we might well keep it in mind that a speaker persuades an audience by the use of stylistic identifications.[67]

If one seeks to persuade his audience by argumentation, he must proceed according to their way of thinking. If he persuades by emotion, he must somehow, sincerely or not, feel the way his audience will be expected to feel. A more obvious example of identification is found, of course, in the speaker who identifies himself more directly with his audience,[68] as a mature man might begin a speech to a group of Boy Scouts by describing the scout troop he belonged to in his day.

Identification has to do, somewhat paradoxically, with division, with partisan aspects of people and ideas. To begin with, it is division and partisanship that provide the situations where identification becomes a human need. And it is only due to the partisan aspects of the social scene that identification, and rhetoric too, have a purpose at all. Identification deals with the pro and con, with one side of a proposition as opposed to the other:

The *Rhetoric* deals with the possibilities of classification in its *partisan* aspects; it considers the ways in which individuals are at odds with one another, or become identified with groups more or less at odds with one another.[69]

[66] *Ibid.*
[68] *Ibid.*, Introduction, p. x.
[67] *Ibid.*, p. 46.
[69] *Ibid.*, p. 22.

And within partisan groups the members share identification with one another. In this sense, rhetoric deals with union and cooperation also. To go further, it needs the dialectic of discussion dealt with in the next section. This gives rhetoric the function of helping discussants in a group come to a residual, mutual compromise that can dissolve partisanship. As Burke says:

Identification is affirmed with earnestness precisely because there is division. Identification is compensatory to division. If men were not apart from one another, there would be no need for the rhetorician to proclaim their unity.[70]

Identification, then, is consubstantiality, belonging. It means the same as persuasion because it covers all that persuasion covers, and yet it goes beyond persuasion in covering the whole field of motivational language, conscious and nonconscious, in the rhetoric of conformity and appeal.[71] Identification is temporarily and topically assuming the rational, emotional, and motivational level of one's audience for the purpose of communicating motivational meaning. It can take many forms. A salesman may identify himself and his product with the client's interests.[72] An orator may seek to have his audience identify themselves with his ideals.[73] An unsuccessful businessman may seek to identify himself with every other unfortunate person who is "not getting the breaks." But the motive words, the pair terms, the vague, fat words that offer such richness of ambiguity, the patterned terms of rationalization, are the implements that make such identification possible.[74] People's daily informal conversations abound with such terms and motivations and never-ending seeking for identification.

HIERARCHY

Hierarchy is Burke's special term for the over-all pattern of these constant and universal strivings after identification. In the

---

[70] *Ibid.*, p. 22.   [71] *Ibid.*, p. 35.   [72] *Ibid.*, p. 46.
[73] *Ibid.*   [74] Burke, *A Grammar of Motives*, pp. 51–53.

present socioeconomic and psychological climate, people are forced to adjust to one another and to cooperate in a way that will bring to the individual and to the group as large a slice as possible of the "good life."[75] The interrelations of people to one another are, in a limited sense, like the structure of a huge pyramid. In the pyramid the blocks in the lowest row are like the people who are most dependent, the next row of blocks may be considered less so, and so on to the top, where the final block has none above it. In this way people are subordinated to one another in a series for every sort of social and economic relationship they have. As Burke remarks in *Counter-Statement*, it is a:

. . . concern with the "pyramidal" nature of social orders, as these affect consciousness and expression. (It concerns the relations that characterize a ladder of Mr. Bigs and Mr. Littles, all along the line, up and down, with the "magic" of these.)[76]

Considering that there are, of course, pyramids within pyramids, there are always people above and people below. There will certainly be a hierarchy, based on incomes, at any country club, but there may also be another hierarchy, based on golf scores. There are hierarchies among school children and among senators. And in each, the individuals all know their places. They know, as they know the means of survival, all the verbalizations, the motive words, the rationalizations that show respect to the individual higher up and display dignity to the one lower down in the pyramid. In all real organizations, social, political, and religious, these same relationships of hierarchy have place, and they make necessary the same motivational activity.

Having examined the linguistic posturing, the rhetorical identifications Burke feels man must make in his strivings for status in his hierarchial order, we can devote a few pages to man's quest for order in artistic expression. The motivation is the same, the identifications go on being made, the rhetoric of strife and of

[75] Burke, *A Rhetoric of Motives*, pp. 137–142.
[76] Burke, *Counter-Statement*, p. 218.

union are still present. But now all these elements are seen at work in a literary context.

THE PHILOSOPHY OF LITERARY FORM

Here Burke treats the nature and kinds of form, the literary symbol, ideology, eloquence, manner, and style.

FORM

There are certain innate and internal patterns of expectancy in the human psychological and psychobiological attitudes. These patterns he calls innate or internal *forms*. They involve basic arrangements or processes like the succession of the seasons, stages of growth, contrast of opposites, and so on.[77] Following these innate expectancies is the pattern of form in style of writing. Burke calls these forms of style or technical forms "an arousing and fulfillment of desires."[78] That is, style has form when it builds us up for an expectancy, with an innate form or pattern, and then answers that expectancy by satisfying it. When the technical form does not follow these patterns of expectancy in some way or other, the literary product can be said to have poor form or no form at all. This is best illustrated by Burke's own example taken from Shakespeare's *Hamlet*.[79] It is not until the fourth scene of Act One that the audience sees the ghost of Hamlet's father, yet for three scenes the form of the play has been employed to prepare them for it and to arouse their desire to see the ghost. Crescendo, balance, repetition, comparison, disclosure, reversal, and magnification are some others of the innate forms upon which Burke bases his technical form.[80]

Burke characterizes five general kinds of form which seem to be applicable to nonliterary as well as literary communication. He calls them Syllogistic Progression, Qualitative Progression, Repetitive Form, Conventional Form, and Minor Form. Syl-

[77] *Ibid.*, pp. 31 and 45–46.
[79] *Ibid.*, pp. 29–30.
[78] *Ibid.*, p. 124.
[80] *Ibid.*, p. 46.

logistic Progression is the step-by-step, logical form of a well-constructed argument.[81] Qualitative Progression is the presence of one quality which prepares the auditor for the introduction of another. Burke's example of this aspect of form is the "grotesque seriousness of the murder scene" (Duncan's murder in *Macbeth*) "preparing us for the grotesque buffoonery of the porter scene."[82] Repetitive Form is "the consistent maintaining of principle under new guises."[83] A series of anecdotes, for example, all restating the same theme or moral, would be an instance of this aspect of form. Conventional Form "involves to some degree the appeal of form as form."[84] It means expecting what categorical convention leads one to expect. The peroration of a speech in formal circumstances, the structure of a sonnet, the soliloquy in Shakespearean drama, are all examples of Conventional Form. Minor Forms are the other incidental expectancies aroused by the artist and satisfied in his auditors. Metaphor and other figures of speech and figures of words are all Minor Forms.[85]

Form is correct, of course, when it does what a form is supposed to do: "Form, having to do with the creation and gratification of needs, is 'correct' insofar as it gratifies the needs it creates."[86] Another thing to be noted is the antithesis between form and information in Burke's theory. When a literary product lacks form, it is usually because it is that type of communication which has as its purpose simply to relate facts as they are.[87] Even though this kind of objective exposition is hardly possible in the strictest purity, present-day science aims at it as an ideal. Between this informational communication and literature of the richest form there can, of course, be literature with varying proportions of both form and information. "There is, obviously, no 'right' proportion of the two."[88] It was the adaptation of rhetoric to this informational trend that was begun with Bacon and has continued more or less uninterruptedly up to the present.

[81] *Ibid.*, p. 124. [82] *Ibid.*, p. 125. [83] *Ibid.*

[84] *Ibid.*, p. 126. [85] *Ibid.*, pp. 127–128. [86] *Ibid.*, p. 138.

[88] *Ibid.*, p. 144. [87] *Ibid.*, pp. 144–146.

THE LITERARY SYMBOL

The literary symbol in Burke's philosophy of style is "the verbal parallel to a pattern of experience."[89] It is the general outline of an experience pattern put into words. The experience must be a familiar one to the readers or hearers, even if only familiar in a smaller application. In this way the symbol of the great Caesar, fallen at the hands of ungrateful friends, the symbol of greatness destroyed by ingratitude, is used by Shakespeare's Mark Antony in his oration over the body of Caesar in *Julius Caesar*. Though readers have not actually experienced this great a calamity, their similar, smaller experiences of ingratitude are frequent and familiar. Similarly, eulogies written after the death of some career man often use the well-worn symbol of the struggle for success, the newsboy-to-president theme.

Symbols of this sort can appeal to readers or listeners in several ways. They can *clarify the characterization* of a novel, the problem of a drama, the issues of pro and con in a political speech. They can *favor the acceptance* of one side of an antithetical choice. They can serve as *compensatory correctives*, as, for instance, where the bustle of city life is fatiguing, a farm-life symbol has the corrective and compensatory appeal of restfulness. Symbols may also *emancipate* the reader from the stricture of his principles by allowing him temporarily to fill the shoes of the literary character who is able to do things which, for the reader, are morally unsuitable.[90]

IDEOLOGY

Symbols are charged with power because of the quasi-universality of the experience pattern they are built upon. "Symbolic intensity arises when the artist uses subject matter 'charged' by the reader's situation outside the work of art."[91] The more common, the more intrinsic to life, the more essential to human need fulfillment this experience is, the more power is charged in the

---

[89] *Ibid.*, p. 152.   [90] *Ibid.*, pp. 154–156.   [91] *Ibid.*, p. 163.

symbol. This charging of symbols has much to do with ideologies. An ideology is simply a general belief or judgment that the artist, orator, or writer can be sure his audience has.[92] The more popular type of newspaper makes use of such ideologies when its news articles on juvenile crime, let us say, imply that teenagers ought to obey and respect their elders; or its news articles on strikes imply two conflicting ideologies, the living wage and the need for public order. A symbol with the appropriate experience pattern and based upon an ideology is charged with considerable power.[93]

ELOQUENCE, MANNER, AND STYLE

Eloquence is the suitable and frequent organized use of these symbolic effects coupled with the effects of form.[94] It calls for a use of much and varied form and a high charge of symbolic power reduplicated by the power of ideology. To relieve the monotony possible to reiterated forms and symbols used to charge expressions, Burke suggests what he calls style. Beyond being the restriction of power stratagems, it strategically modifies and arranges them so as to produce "saliency."[95] To restrict, in turn, the excess of variety and complexity of form and symbol, Burke proposes manner.[96] These concepts of style and manner seem restrictive until it becomes apparent that Burke means the entire faculty of literary judgment in operation for the author as he composes. It is style and manner that tell him what to put where and how much.

Manner obviously has the virtue of "power," with the danger of monotony . . . . Style has the virtue of "complexity," with the danger of diffusion.[97]

For the culmination of Burke's rhetoric of motivation, the principles and guideposts designed to direct us to personal and global harmony, with a happier use of symbols, we must wait for

[92] *Ibid.*, pp. 161–163.
[93] *Ibid.*, pp. 163–165.
[94] *Ibid.*, pp. 165–166.
[95] *Ibid.*, pp. 165–167.
[96] *Ibid.*, pp. 166–167.
[97] *Ibid.*, p. 167.

the publication of the two works that promise to complete his study of symbolism.

SOME INSTRUMENTAL APPLICATIONS OF BURKE'S THEORY

Like Richards, Burke has not only evolved a fairly complete philosophy of rhetoric, but he has, in his philosophizing, worked out practical instruments to be applied to a consciously improved use of rhetoric for writing and speaking, reading and listening. Among these instrumental applications are three that deserve to be pointed up as important elements in the culmination of Burke's theory. They are his pentad format, his system of index-ing, and his precautions about naming and labelling. These ele-ments are to receive fuller consideration in their extension to teaching rhetoric in Chapter 5, but at this point a brief descrip-tion of their practical functions will give direction to the more philosophic elements of Burke's theory.

The *pentad format* has a universality of application that makes it practical for the functions of interpretation of communi-cation, the search for the most meaningful motivations in a sym-bolic utterance, and even the solving of any theoretical problem where research is possible.[98] The fundamental secret of its effi-ciency is that it not only asks searching questions, but that it asks them all.[99] It manages, as Richards managed in his seven instru-ments, to include all the possible questions, somehow, in its five wide classifications of inquiry. When one has answered all five questions, he has answered, in the context of his problem, all the questions pertinent to the problem. Refinements and branch in-quiries are, of course, always possible. When they are proposed, they will usually fit into one or more of the five classifications of the pentad.

As applied to interpretation, the function of the pentad as a set of measuring instruments and its likeness to other similar in-

[98] Burke, *A Grammar of Motives*, Introduction, pp. xv–xvi.
[99] *Ibid.*, p. 340.

struments like those of Richards and Lasswell are clear from what has been said above. But as a device for separating the more and the less meaningful motivations beneath rhetorical language, it does its best work. Burke is full of examples of this sort of application of the pentad.[100] In particular, *A Grammar of Motives*, the work that introduced the pentad, contains lengthy samples of literary analysis based on the asking of these five questions and always finding what is, at least for Burke, the fuller motivational significance of the literary passage.

Burke's *system of indexing* is a detailed method of analyzing the "internality,"[101] or motivational meaning, of a lengthy communication. It watches for key words, or "linguistic facts,"[102] in the work to be indexed. Then it compares these key words, using the different literary contexts in which they reappear, so as to find the deeper motivational significance lying beneath the writer's literary devices and the richer dimensions of meaning and of unity in the entire work of art. Perhaps, by stringing together some of Burke's terms, a brief and adequate description of this system may be provided: thus indexing comes to be "systematic . . . concordance" of "key terms" or "terministic facts" of a written work "to make clear all elements of inference or interpretation" and "offer a rationale" for them by "studying the 'facts' " of each such identical term as it "recurs in changing contexts."[103]

The key terms in *Hamlet* might include the words "father," "decision," "avenge," and so on. And a Burkeian index would seek out all their contexts, note the shades of differences in each, shuffle and shake them, look at them again and again from his multiple points of view, and finally come to the most reasonable

[100] *Ibid.*, pp. 33–35 and 53–55. Burke often exemplifies this method in the shape of an internal argument as in *Permanence and Change*, pp. 161 ff. and 175–178.

[101] Kenneth Burke, "Fact, Inference, and Proof in the Analysis of Literary Symbolism," in *Symbols and Values: An Initial Study*, ed. Lyman Bryson, Louis Finkelstein, R. M. MacIver, and Richard McKeon (New York: Harper & Brothers, 1954), p. 298.

[102] *Ibid.*, pp. 283–284.   [103] *Ibid.*, pp. 283–287.

conclusion as to meaning and motivation. But Burke provides several other samples of his application of this system. His analysis of James Joyce's *A Portrait of the Artist as a Young Man*[104] is his own explicit vehicle for explaining the system of indexing. He has applied the index in several analyses of Freud's writings and gives his readers the results of such studies in *The Philosophy of Literary Form*[105] and *A Rhetoric of Motives.*[106]

One of the important elements in this system is the necessity of searching for the stages of development of the meaning as the units of the index pile up.[107] Another is the way the insight caught by the index moves from particularizing to generalizing as it develops.[108] Then, too, at the end of any unified section or complete part of a work, the indexer is able to crystallize the resultants of the index by naming the section for the meaning and motivation he has found. This is a type of classroom exercise which Burke has used with success during the past few years. He calls it "essentializing by entitlement."[109]

Of importance to the concept of index are Burke's ten hints or admonitions to the indexer:

1. Note all striking terms for acts, ideas, attitudes, images, relationships.
2. Note oppositions.
3. Pay particular attention to beginnings and endings of sections or subsections.

[104] *Ibid.,* pp. 283–306.
[105] Burke, *The Philosophy of Literary Form,* pp. 258–292.
[106] Burke, *A Rhetoric of Motives,* pp. 294–298.
[107] Burke, in *Symbols and Values: An Initial Study,* p. 290.
[108] *Ibid.,* pp. 292–293.
[109] For example, in a teaching situation, Burke would suggest to students applying his index system that they give titles to the acts of a play, or to the parts of a novel, or to the stanzas of a poem, in order to force themselves to decide what might be the essence of each step of the total development of the play, novel, or poem. Where such titles are already given in the work to be indexed, students can be asked to offer alternative titles (for instance, a specific title where a general one is already given, or vice versa). From an interview with Kenneth Burke, New York, May 29, 1957.

4. Watch names, as indicative of essence.
5. Watch also for incidental properties of one character that are present in another.
6. Note internal forms.
7. Watch for a point of *farthest internality*.
8. Note details of *scene* that may stand "astrologically" for motivations affecting character, or for some eventual act in which that character will complete himself.
9. Note expressions marking secrecy, privacy, mystery, marvel, power, silence, guilt.
10. Look for *moments* at which, in your opinion, the work comes to *fruition*.[110]

These ten admonitions, with emphasis upon the last as the entelechial test, are primarily useful in the best selection of key terms for the compiling of the index.

Burke's *precautions about naming and labelling* take on practical significance when applied to some distinct areas of terminology. The growing availability of psychiatric analysis and other forms of professional assistance to the mentally disturbed has brought the terminology of psychiatry into the everyday vocabulary of the common man. *Oedipus* and *inferiority complexes, analysis, rationalization, escape, persecution, substitution, sublimation, frustration,* and *therapy* have become household words. Burke's point about all this is that these are symbols with certain motivation content as used in different situations.[111] So, in fairness to the people and situations about which they are used, they need careful examination by means of the pentad format or, in longer communications, with the system of indexing. Having made such examinations himself,[112] Burke feels that the application of such terms to a mental patient's disturbance does little more than institute a new naming system for him. This "secular conversion,"[113] as Burke terms it, is meant to give the patient a

[110] Burke, in *Symbols and Values: An Initial Study*, pp. 296–303.
[111] Burke, *Permanence and Change*, pp. 23–24.
[112] For an example of this process applied to Freudian psychoanalysis, see Burke, *The Philosophy of Literary Form*, pp. 258–292.
[113] Burke, *op. cit.*, p. 125.

whole new orientation. He feels that the patient facing this new orientation is no more facing reality than he was before, because the new terms for his illness are just a new set of motive symbols. If he was rationalizing with his old orientation, then he is still rationalizing with the new terminology.[114] For Burke, though, rationalizing is not a dishonest fabrication whereby a noble motive is substituted for a meaner one. Neither is it a conscious, subconscious, or unconscious self-deception in the sense of the psychoanalysts. It is simply a statement in terms of current social conventions of why it was done.

Our objection to the psycho-analytic emphasis is that it would tend to accuse a man of self-deceptive rationalization if diagnosing his hunger motive as an altruistic motive, whereas any set of motives is but part of a larger implicit or explicit rationalization regarding human purpose as a whole.[115]

Burke accepts rationalization as a natural process. It is the attempt to raise it to the conscious level and examine it that interests him. He sees it not really as a motive in the agent, but as a statement of the scene of the act in question plus a name for the particular kind of scene that made the agent perform the act. As he says,

Often one thinks he has a motive in the agent, when actually he has two terms for scene as motive, one being the term that on its face is situational, the other being a class-name for that *kind* of situation. Thus, "The man, being pursued, ran through fear," would, in substance, be: "The man, in a fear situation, ran through fear."[116]

Burke seems to feel that the psychoanalysts who explain away a problem by saying it is due to an Oedipus complex or a father image are in effect just making another rationalization.[117] What

[114] Burke, *Permanence and Change*, pp. 125–129, 17–18, 23–25, and 35–36.

[115] *Ibid.*, p. 26.

[116] From Burke's notes commenting on the first draft of this summary, Andover, New Jersey, December 22, 1956.

[117] Burke, *Permanence and Change*, p. 23.

happens, in Burke's view, during the psychoanalytic therapy of conversion is the lifting of a human problem out of its complicated human situation where there are no answers to it, and the relocating of it in a scientific situation where the answers are close to hand.[118] Burke's objection is that this relocation of the problem cannot take place without a shift of circumference. The curative effect of the therapy then, in this analysis, would be due not to the application of scientific principle, but to the provision of a new and rich source of rationalization.[119]

Burke's instrumental applications bring us to the completion of this summary of his philosophy of rhetoric, and we can now turn to the third theory, that of the General Semanticists.

[118] *Ibid.*, p. 125.　　　　　　[119] *Ibid.*, pp. 125–129.

CHAPTER 4

The General Semantics Theory

THE THIRD PHILOSOPHY OF RHETORIC COMES FROM A GROUP OF scholars and teachers of mathematics, English, speech, and speech therapy who in the last twenty-five years have come to be known as General Semanticists. Their conception of rhetoric has different sources, aims, and direction from the theories of Richards and Burke, even though they arrive at many points in common with them. Unlike Richards and Burke, they lay claim to a completely empirical foundation and method. Their emphasis seems predominantly therapeutic—to cure our mental ills through the application of science to our uses of language. Richards and Burke, on the other hand, while recognizing the linguistic factor in personal balance, direct our attention primarily to the wonderful complexity of our language and to ways to live with that complexity. General Semantics expressly and repeatedly terms its theory "non-Aristotelian" because it advocates a new and scientific language consistent with our non-Euclidean, scientific age.

Such points of comparison with the other two theories and with the traditional theory of rhetoric will come into stronger light as this summary proceeds.

It is important to consider the spokesmanship for this theory as coming from a group of scholars rather than from any one man's thinking. The ideas of the late Alfred Korzybski, the founder of "General Semantics," form the background and point of departure for the movement's philosophy of rhetoric. The works of S. I. Hayakawa, of Irving J. Lee, and of Wendell Johnson point toward applications of General Semantics to educational purposes.

Alfred Korzybski was a Polish-born mathematician and engineer who came to this country after serving with the Intelligence Staff of the Second Russian Army in World War I. He first published his theories in *The Manhood of Humanity* (1921), but they came to a more mature culmination in his master work, *Science and Sanity* (1933). In 1935 Korzybski organized the First American Congress on General Semantics, and three years later founded the Institute of General Semantics in Chicago, to further what had by then become not only a theory but an organization.[1] Among the first of the enthusiastic followers of the new movement was a young instructor at the University of Wisconsin, Samuel I. Hayakawa. Within three years of the founding of the Institute, he had published a popular version of the General Semantics theory as applied to educational purposes. *Language in Action* (1941) was written as a doctoral dissertation at the University of Wisconsin and intended as base for an experimental alternate for English composition on the University campus and in the off-campus extension centers. It was selected by the Book-of-the-Month Club and became a best seller. In text editions, it achieved still wider distribution for use in first-year

[1] Alfred Korzybski, *Science and Sanity* (3rd ed. rev.; Lakeville, Conn.: The International Non-Aristotelian Library Publishing Co., 1948), Introduction to 2nd ed., pp. x–xi.

courses in many colleges and universities.[2] A revised and expanded version, *Language in Thought and Action* (1949), though not commonly referred to as such, is for the most part a philosophy of rhetoric.

Numerous other scholars in various fields have written extensively of applications of General Semantics in modern society —Anatole Rapoport, a mathematical biologist: *Science and the Goals of Man* (1950) and *Operational Philosophy* (1953); and Stuart Chase, lecturer and economist: *The Tyranny of Words* (1938), *The Power of Words* (1954), and *Guides to Straight Thinking* (1956)—to mention two whose works have been given wide publicity.[3] But there are two others whose work points more specifically toward rhetoric—Wendell Johnson and Irving J. Lee. Wendell Johnson, educated at Iowa University, and professor of speech pathology and psychology there since 1945, began to use General Semantics methods to help cure speech defects and failures. His widely known work, *People in Quandaries* (1946), provides a brief description of the general Korzybskian principles before applying them to preventive and curative therapy for speech problems that lead to personal maladjustment.[4] The late Irving J. Lee, professor of speech at Northwestern University until 1956, experimented with ways of using General Semantics to improve human relations in business and industry and in group procedures in education. His *Language Habits in Human Affairs* (1941) and *How to Talk with People* (1952), along with his extensive lecturing and consultant services, point toward a new rhetoric for conference and compromise.[5]

The General Semantics theory, therefore, will be treated under five heads: the Korzybskian background of the theory, the

[2] Interview with S. I. Hayakawa, New York, May 28, 1957.

[3] S. I. Hayakawa, *Language, Meaning and Maturity* (New York: Harper & Brothers, 1954), pp. 4–5.

[4] Wendell Johnson, *People in Quandaries* (New York: Harper & Brothers, 1946), Introduction, pp. x–xi.

[5] Irving J. Lee, *How to Talk with People* (New York: Harper & Brothers, 1952), Introduction, pp. ix–xiv.

theory of abstraction, the epistemological theory, the theory of definition, and the instrumental applications of Korzybski, Hayakawa, Lee, and Johnson.

THE KORZYBSKIAN BACKGROUND

Man, Korzybski argues, learned his method of structuring thoughts into words and sentences in prescientific times. His thought and language habits were appropriately prescientific in a prescientific age.[6] But that adolescent stage in man's historic growth has passed. He has reached maturity in the present scientific age. With the more recent discoveries in mathematics, physics, biochemistry, psychology, and psychiatry, man has come to his manhood. But in his scientific maturity he needs a new scientific language. He needs a new way of structuring his thoughts into words and sentences that takes into account all the new things he has found out.[7]

THE "ORGANISM-AS-A-WHOLE" PRINCIPLE

To find this new language, or linguistic method, Korzybski turns to the sciences that have created the need for it. From experiments with colloids and studies of the simpler animals, he reaches his first and probably basic principle. He calls it the "organism-as-a-whole" principle.[8] When any part of an organism experiences a stimulus, the whole organism is affected by it. There is a Gestalt quality to the cooperation of all the complex parts of the organism to make one unified response.[9] In colloids, which are emulsions or suspensions of submicroscopic solids or liquids in a gaseous or liquid medium, the electric charges between positives and negatives keep the suspended particles from cohering and crystallizing into a complete coagulation. Surface

---

[6] Korzybski, *op. cit.*, pp. xlviii–xlix.
[7] *Ibid.*, Preface to 1st ed., pp. lxviii–lxix.
[8] *Ibid.*, pp. 101, 111–122, and 123–130.   [9] *Ibid.*, pp. 123–124.

tension, working in the other direction, tends to make the particles unite to reduce tension and promote coagulation.[10] Organic colloids, when stimulated by an electric charge, not only react as a whole to the stimulus, but they do so with a special rapidity:

In inorganic colloids, an electrical current does not coagulate the whole, but only that portion of it within the immediate vicinity of the electrodes. Not so in living protoplasm. Even a weak current usually coagulates the entire protoplasm, because the inter-cellular films probably play the role of electrodes and so the entire protoplasm structurally represents the "immediate vicinity" of the electrodes. Similarly, structure also accounts for the extremely rapid spread of some effects upon the whole of the organism.[11]

Experiments with simple animals like the earthworm and certain types of marine life provide Korzybski with proof of the wholeness of the organic response in living things. Tiny eggs sometimes develop without actually being fertilized by a spermatozoon. Often they develop into larvae simply because the chemical solution in the surrounding water changes, or because they are punctured with a needle.[12]

In so many experiments a stimulus partly similar to the generative stimulus seems to start the organism off on the complete and intricately cooperative process of reproduction.

Since our bodies are made up of various systems of colloidal structure, Korzybski feels that any energy potentials in the body—feelings, emotions, thoughts—affect these structures and the human organism as a whole. So stimuli from linguistic symbols have a rapidly spreading effect upon the whole human organism:

Under such environmental conditions, we must take into account all energies which have been discovered, *semantic reactions not excluded,* as all such energies have structural effect. As language is one of the expressions of one of these energies, we ought to find it quite natural that the structure of language finds its reflection in the structure of the environmental conditions which are dependent on it.[13]

[10] *Ibid.,* p. 112.   [11] *Ibid.,* p. 115.   [12] *Ibid.,* pp. 123–124.
[13] *Ibid.,* p. 121.

By studying reactions of living nerve tissue and finding that the responses are more specialized and complex in the higher types of animals, Korzybski sees the implications for humans in the stimuli of linguistic symbols. Further experimentation with the effects of deficiencies in nutrition upon persons suffering from so-called mental and nervous diseases indicated that the whole human organism often responds in its habitual ways to the stimulus it "thinks" is there, even when it is not. The hay-fever sufferer who has a severe attack on the sudden appearance of a bouquet of paper roses is a case in point. As Korzybski says:

Empirical data show clearly that the most diversified factors, acting as partial stimuli, ultimately affect or result in the response of the whole.[14]

When these diversified factors act as partial stimuli with linguistic symbols, the receiver may get the wrong or incomplete semantic message, and the upsetting consequences reach the whole organism. From the findings of modern psychiatry Korzybski concludes that the semantic difficulties of some patients can be treated with semantic or linguistic cures and preventatives, that illness rooted in disturbed communication can be cured by restructuring our patterns of communication.

The handling of such empirical, structural, fundamental problems involves serious structural, linguistic, and semantic difficulties which have to be solved *entirely* by adjusting the structure of the language used.[15]

It is this that sets Korzybski on the hunt for a new organism-as-a-whole or nonelementalistic language that will be in keeping with the age of science and hence will preserve our mental health.

The *non-el* [nonelementalistic] principle formulates a structural character inherently found in the structure of the world, ourselves, and

---

[14] *Ibid.*, p. 129.   [15] *Ibid.*

our nervous systems on all levels; the knowledge and application of which is unconditionally necessary for adjustment at all levels, and, therefore, in humans, for *sanity*.[16]

Quite clearly, for Korzybski, the only way to set up the new, nonelementalistic, organism-as-a-whole terminology is to study the intimate relational structures of language, clear away what is elementalistic, and coin new nonelementalistic terms. He would build a language whose structure corresponds to the structure found experimentally in nature. Then semantic stimuli true to reality would promote healthful stimulus-response conditions, because they would be free of the deceptive quality of the old, faulty language structure:

As "knowledge," "understanding," and such functions are *solely* relational, and, therefore, structural, the unconditional and inherent condition for adjustment on all human levels depends on building languages of similar structure to the experimental facts. Once this is accomplished, all the former desirable semantic consequences will follow automatically.[17]

From this position Korzybski goes into the fundamentals of language structure, the abstracting process, and the elements of a theory of definition.

Korzybski's *structural differential* is his graphic illustration of his conception of the abstracting process.[18] In the accompanying Figure 5, the parabola (A) represents the actual event outside our skins which stimulates our nervous systems. The curve and the broken edge at the top (B) signify the magnitude and extent of the event, with its infinite number of characteristics represented by the small holes (C). The large circle (O) stands for the object *as perceived* by the nervous system. Its characteristics (the small holes [C']) are finite and fewer because the nervous system cannot perceive all the infinity of characteristics actually in the real event. The rectangular part beneath the ob-

[16] *Ibid.*, p. 130.   [17] *Ibid.*   [18] *Ibid.*, pp. 386–411.

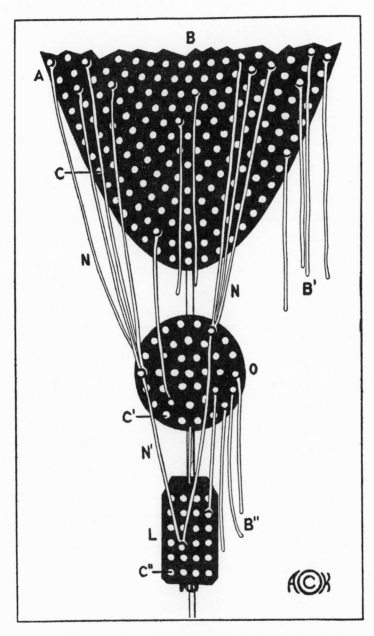

FIGURE 5—KORZYBSKI'S "STRUCTURAL DIFFERENTIAL." From *Science and Sanity*, by Alfred Korzybski (International Non-Aristotelian Library Publishing Company, Third Edition, 1948), p. 388. Used by permission.

ject represents the next stage of abstraction, the label (L) or word that goes with the event. Korzybski pegs some of the characteristics C″ to indicate which ones are perceived and which left out in the first stage of abstraction:

The nervous process of abstracting we represent by the lines (N), (N′). The characteristics *left out*, or not abstracted, are indicated by the lines (B′), (B″).[19]

In other words, some of the characteristics of the stimulus are not abstracted in each step of the process and consequently do not get carried forward to become a part of the further stimulus in the next step of the abstraction. The loose hanging strings (B′) and (B″) are the characteristics that are left out or not abstracted.

To the label "pencil" we would ascribe, perhaps, its length, thickness, shape, colour, hardness. But we would mostly *disregard* the accidental characteristics, such as a scratch on its surface . . . .[20]

The tied strings (N) and (N′) represent the characteristics abstracted and carried forward as stimuli to the next step in the process. The norm of selection and rejection in this process is, of course, the special motivation of the person abstracting.[21] The operation can go on and on indefinitely with an unlimited number of rectangles standing for higher and higher orders of abstraction, but always losing characteristics with each new level of abstraction.[22] Thus the label or definition of the object has fewer characteristics than the object, even as represented to our consciousness by our nervous system. And the object itself has fewer characteristics in turn than the actual event.[23] These steps between the event and the perceived object and the label require separate steps in the process of abstraction:

We must consider the object as a "first abstraction" (with a finite number of characteristics) from the infinite numbers of characteristics an event has . . . .

[19] *Ibid.*, p. 389. [20] *Ibid.*, p. 387. [21] *Ibid.*
[22] *Ibid.*, p. 392. [23] *Ibid.*, p. 387.

The label, the *importance* of which lies in its *meanings to us,* represents a still higher abstraction from the event, and usually labels, also, a *semantic reaction.*[24]

THE MULTIORDINAL RELATIONS PRINCIPLE

The *multiordinal relations principle* requires that language-users not forget the multifaceted and infinite characteristics they necessarily leave out when they abstract. When people use the "is" of identity to connect as identical two real things, they cannot be correct because they cannot possibly know the infinite complexity of all the characteristics of the real event which were left out in the first level of abstraction.[25] One can easily be conscious of leaving out characteristics if the terms are the kind that are used on all orders and levels of abstraction almost at will. Such terms are so commonly used for well-known different meanings that it is easier to be aware of the shift of their meaning when they are used in a different order or level of abstraction. Such are "multiordinal" terms:

The main characteristic of these terms consists of the fact that on different levels of orders of abstractions they may have different meanings, with the result that they have no general meaning; for their meanings are determined solely by the given context, which establishes the different orders of abstractions.[26]

Examples of multiordinal terms may be found among the central terms of the Korsybskian system: "multiordinal," "structure," "relation," "extension," "orientation," "non-Aristotelian," "nonelementalistic," and, in fact, any "non" term, are examples. They all indicate an applicability and relativity that ensure them against leaving out any, or many, of the important relational characteristics of the real things they symbolize.[27] Nor will they even limit the "structures" of thought we build in the sciences in accordance with the structures really existing in nature.[28]

[24]*Ibid.,* p. 389.
[25]*Ibid.,* pp. 388–389 and 416.
[26]*Ibid.,* p. 14.
[27]*Ibid.,* pp. 433–434.
[28]*Ibid.,* pp. 436 and 63–64.

Roots for a New Rhetoric

The final facet of this principle of General Semantics contends that since words (as in Richards' theory) are not things and things are far too complex and rich to be expressed by words in any adequately factual way, we must not only use a new terminology, but we must spend the energies of our intellects examining the "structures" we can observe in things themselves and in our relations to things.[29] In other words, we cannot express the fullness of things, or even any one thing, in verbal symbols. But we can express the nature of the relationships, the "structures," we see in them. Korzybski concerns himself particularly with two classifications of relations.

These two classifications have to do with symmetry and with transition. The first classification he divides into symmetrical, nonsymmetrical, and asymmetrical. Korzybski uses the symbols "A" and "B" and "C" for the things between which the relationships exist. A relation between A and B which also holds between B and A is called *symmetrical* (the relation "spouse"). *Nonsymmetrical* relations are those that hold between A and B but *not necessarily* between B and A, as when we say, "A is the brother of B." (Here B is not necessarily a brother of A; B could be the sister of A.) *Asymmetrical* relations are those that hold between A and B and can never hold between B and A (as in the case of the relationship of "father"). If A is father to B, then B can never have a father relationship to A.[30]

The second classification is divided into transitive, nontransitive, and intransitive relations. They deal with three or more things to be related. They are *transitive* when they hold between A and B and between B and C and also hold between A and C (for example, A may have the relation of being "before" B; similarly B is "before" C; and it is still true that A is before C). Nontransitive relations hold between A and B, and between B and C, but *not necessarily* between A and C (the relation of "dissimilarity" is a case in point—if A is dissimilar to B, and B is dissimilar to C, it does not follow that A is dissimilar to C). Rela-

[29] *Ibid.*, p. 29.   [30] *Ibid.*, pp. 188–193.

98

tions that hold between *A* and *B*, and between *B* and *C*, and *never* hold between *A* and *C* are called *intransitive* relations (the relation of "father" is a clear example of this).[31]

Most of the varieties of relations treated in the philosophies can be included under these very general relations of Korzybski. Cause and effect, spatial, geometric, and numerical proportion relations, as well as qualitative and quantitative comparison relations, are evidently included here. The importance of these relations resides in the contention that such relationships and their "structures" make up the whole of our knowledge. We do not really know *things*, it is argued, we only know the "structures" and relationships *in* and *between* things.[32]

THE INTENSIONAL–EXTENSIONAL PRINCIPLE

The *intensional–extensional principle* states, and with evident dependence upon the other two principles, that one's attitude toward things and relations ought to be *extensional* as opposed to *intensional*. That is, it should seek the real as opposed to the mental; the physically extant in four dimensions as opposed to the imaginal, ideal, or intellectual presence of a thought in the mind; the documentation from "outside our skin" as opposed to processes "inside our skin."[33] In addition, the term "extension" carries the notion of empirical enumeration. An "extensional" definition of a group of men, for instance, would require, in Korzybski's terminology, a description or naming of each of the individuals in the group (John Jones, Bill Smith, etc.). The "intensional" definition would find some quality that was common to all the individuals and thus classify them (several golfers).[34] In this way the "extensional" definition, as also the "extensional" term or relation, or "structure," limits or denotes the individual and describes him only by empirical examination of the individual himself. It describes his class only by an examination of each in-

[31] *Ibid.*, pp. 189–190.
[32] *Ibid.*, pp. 20 and 130.
[33] *Ibid.*, pp. 173–174.   [34] *Ibid.*, p. 173.

dividual in that class, and never by "mere" abstraction or a priori reasoning, as happens in "intensional" defining.[35]

We can now turn to Hayakawa who adapts General Semantics as a philosophy of rhetoric for the classroom. He underwrites all that Korzybski says, but adds his "ladder of abstraction," his English teacher's approach to metaphor, and his educational approaches to epistemology and definition.

THE THEORY OF ABSTRACTION

Under this heading we discuss three items: Hayakawa's "ladder of abstraction," consciousness of abstracting, and figures of speech. Korzybski's structural differential is itself a high order of abstraction, perhaps even of an "intensional" sort. Hayakawa seeks to put its principles into daily idiom with his simplification which he calls an abstraction ladder (see Figure 6).[36]

The lowest level in the process (I) is the extensional cow. This is the thing with which the abstraction process is concerned.[37] The following level (II), the first abstractive step, is the human perceptional sorting stage that is not yet linguistic and provides no word for Bessie. But one can experience her through nervous reactions, just like the earthworms and jellyfish in Korzybski's studies, except that they could not take the further steps up the "abstraction ladder" as a human can. It is a kind of reaction to a stimulus whereby the organism, whether amoeba or man, is not merely physically affected by the stimulus (as a stone is affected by being pushed aside), but itself, as a whole organism, goes through an integrating process which results in a fundamentally changed organism.[38] The next level (III) is the specifically Korzybskian level. Here is the difference between the

[35] *Ibid.*

[36] S. I. Hayakawa, *Language in Thought and Action* (New York: Harcourt, Brace & Co., 1949), p. 169. A slight change has been made in Hayakawa's "ladder" (see facing page) to make clear the difference between his and the traditional theory.

[37] *Ibid.*, p. 167.   [38] *Ibid.*

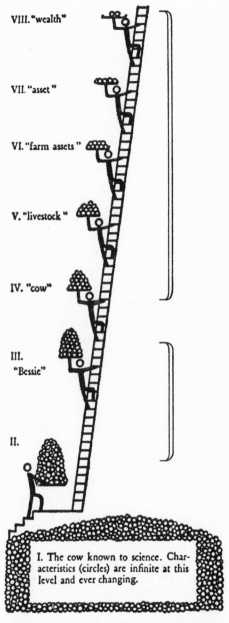

VIII. "wealth"

VII. "asset"

VI. "farm assets"

V. "livestock"

IV. "cow"

III.
"Bessie"

II.

I. The cow known to science. Characteristics (circles) are infinite at this level and ever changing.

The levels of abstraction as usually understood in the older, traditional logic and epistemology. The higher the abstraction the fewer characteristics and the more numerous the objects represented.

Step III in the process is peculiar to the General Semanticists—the "label" step. Though it still represents only one object, it has fewer characteristics than step II.

This is the first order (I) or level of abstraction possible to almost all forms of life. It is also termed primordial abstraction or perception.

FIGURE 6—MODIFICATION OF HAYAKAWA'S "ABSTRACTION LADDER." (*Read up.*) From *Language in Thought and Action*, by S. I. Hayakawa (Harcourt, Brace & Co., 1949), p. 169. Used by permission.

present theory and the theory of the other philosophies of rhetoric. The step where the abstracter reacts to Bessie in language is made a special level of abstraction.

When we say, then, that "Bessie is a cow," we are only noting the process-Bessie's resemblance to other "cows" and ignoring differences. What is more we are leaping a huge chasm: from the dynamic process-Bessie, a whirl of electro-chemico-neural eventfulness, to a relatively static "idea," "concept," or *word*, "cow."[39]

As we shall see below in the treatment of the General Semantics epistemology, the word is not the thing, the word "Bessie" is not the real cow. So, to cross the chasm between the real and the verbal, we need a special order or level of abstraction.

Perhaps the subsequent steps or orders of the process are clear enough, since they become, with the fourth order and the following orders, the same in this connection as the traditional, Aristotelian process of abstraction. This process means the selection of a certain characteristic occurring in a number of real things, and giving that abstracted or separated characteristic a name.[40] Thus we can observe the characteristic "white" as seeming to occur in a piece of paper, a wall, and a glass of milk. We can mentally separate this characteristic for consideration and call it "whiteness." The other, higher abstractions simply pare off more and more characteristics until Hayakawa gets to "wealth," or we go farther and get "thing."[41]

The *consciousness of abstracting* is perhaps its most important aspect for the General Semanticists, because it helps prevent the confusion of orders or levels of abstraction:

The consciousness of abstracting eliminates *automatically* identification or "confusion of the orders of abstraction," both applying to the semantic confusion on all levels. If we are *not* conscious of abstracting, we are bound to identify or confuse the object with its finite number of characteristics, with the event, with its infinite num-

---

[39] *Ibid.*, p. 167.   [40] *Ibid.*, pp. 168–170.   [41] *Ibid.*, p. 167.

bers of *different* characteristics. Confusion of these levels may misguide us into semantic situations ending in unpleasant shocks.[42]

Figures of speech, in the General Semantics theory, are closely connected with abstraction. Metaphor, for instance, is the abstracting of a characteristic from one reality and coupling it with another reality in a symbolic expression.

One of the useful functions of metaphor is its tendency to enrich the language with new terms. The metaphor in "the leg of the table" has long since lost its literary imagery and become a normal term in the language for indicating that part of the table.

Metaphor is probably the most important of all the means by which language develops, changes, grows, and adapts itself to our changing needs. When metaphors are successful, they "die"—that is, they become so much a part of our regular language that we cease thinking of them as metaphors at all.[43]

The emphasis here is on the validity and usefulness of the metaphor as an affective mechanism of communication. It is not merely a style device but an instrument of affective expression.

Metaphors are not "ornaments of discourse"; they are direct expressions of evaluations and are bound to occur whenever we have strong feelings to express.[44]

. . . . .

Metaphor, simile, and personification are among the most useful communicative devices we have, because by their quick affective power they often make unnecessary the inventing of new words for new things or new feelings.[45]

This reduplicated description of abstraction as both Hayakawa and Korzybski see it may help to make clearer the subsequent summary of the General Semantics epistemological theory.

[42] Korzybski, *op. cit.,* p. 417.
[43] Hayakawa, *Language in Thought and Action,* p. 124.
[44] *Ibid.,* p. 121.   [45] *Ibid.,* p. 123.

THE EPISTEMOLOGICAL THEORY

For the purposes of this summary it will be convenient to sum up the logic and epistemology of this theory in three principles: the "nonidentity" principle, the "multiordinal relations" principle, and the "intensional–extensional" principle. In the linear order of discussion of these three principles, there is no implication that they are adequately distinct from one another, that they do not overlap, or that they are not sometimes corollaries of one another.

The *nonidentity principle* has to do with the relationship between the subject and object of a proposition when they are joined by the verb "to be." For Korzybski and Hayakawa and other General Semanticists, the essential flaw in the Aristotelian system is the use of the "is" of identity in this circumstance.[46] When we say, "This is a pencil," the statement is unconditionally false to facts, because the object appears as an absolute individual and *is not* words.[47] Korzybski means that nothing said or written, no word or symbol or description can *be* the extended, physically real pencil. For him, it is impossible to cross the line from the verbal, symbolic order to the real, physical, extended order via the "is" of identity. Nothing in the verbal order can possibly be identical with anything in the real order. To avoid this flaw which, he feels, creates a "semantic blockage,"[48] Korzybski suggests the use of the strictly predicative "is," which does not try to connect by identity, does not try to say what a thing is, but rather says something about it.[49] He further suggests that the negative "is" is valid and true to fact for general use:

Say whatever you choose *about* the object, and whatever you might say *is not* it. Or, in other words; Whatever you might say the object "is," well it *is not*. This negative statement is *final* because it is *negative*.[50]

---

[46] Korzybski, *op. cit.*, pp. 34–35.   [47] *Ibid.*, p. 35.
[48] *Ibid.*, p. 18.   [49] *Ibid.*, p. 93.   [50] *Ibid.*, p. 35.

He seems to intend that the denying of the "is" of identity by the "not" makes it true to fact. And the reason why it is true to fact is that it denies a falsehood, the falsehood of the "is" of identity.

Hayakawa makes what might be considered a further concession. In dealing with this principle, he concedes that the identity relationship between subject and predicate may have very valid uses so long as everyone who uses it is agreed upon what it really means and how it is to be used:

Generally speaking, I have made the swing with Wendell Johnson away from a revolution in terms towards a revolution in *semantical reactions* [italics added]. I feel that there are certain inexact expressions we use in ordinary conversation that are perfectly all right so long as everybody understands them as inexact. One may say with no danger of misinterpretation, for instance, that "the sun rises" though, of course, it doesn't really rise at all.[51]

Hayakawa explains this seeming deflection from the usual severity of the "nonidentity" principle by reminding his readers that this, while it does use the old, outdated, "two-valued"[52] orientation, does not, in these instances, attempt to cross the line from verbal things to real things and so has not the usual flaw of the "is" of identity: "Logic is language about language, not language about things or events,"[53] he says, in an attempt to show that the "is" of identity may be usable also in some logical and mathematical formulae which keep their whole content in the verbal, linguistic, and logical order and never cross over into the area where they begin to establish identity between these logical, verbal entities and real extended things.[54]

THE THEORY OF DEFINITION

The following passage from Hayakawa is his opening paragraph on definition. It clearly summarizes the General Semantics position:

[51] Interview with S. I. Hayakawa, New York, May 28, 1957.
[52] Hayakawa, *Language and Thought in Action*, p. 235.
[53] *Ibid.*, p. 240.   [54] *Ibid.*, pp. 239–240.

Definitions, contrary to popular opinion, tell us nothing about things. They only describe people's linguistic habits; that is, they tell us what noises people make under what conditions. Definitions could be understood as *statements about language*.[55]

The General Semantics definitional position can be discussed as defining with the "abstraction ladder."

Hayakawa uses his "abstraction ladder" again to make clear what he has to say about definitions. In short, he suspects them. He feels that they should be used as little as possible, or else be cut down to where they "point to extensional levels wherever necessary—and in writing and speaking, this means giving specific examples of what we are talking about."[56] The main reason for the suspicion of definitions is that definers often define by using terms of the same abstraction level in the definition, which, for him and other General Semanticists, means not coming down from the abstractive levels to concrete things, and so, not really pointing out the things themselves. By "pointing to extensional levels" he means, of course, pointing one's definition downward on the "abstraction ladder" so that the definition gets, eventually, to concrete objects.[57] Another basic difficulty with definitions is that, with some people, they tend to go up the "ladder" rather than down, and end up in what are, for General Semanticists at least, impossibly abstract and unreal generalizations.

If, on the other hand, we habitually go down the abstraction ladder to lower levels of abstraction when we are asked the meaning of a word, we are less likely to get lost in verbal mazes.[58]

Finally, definitions seem to the General Semanticist to lead most often to a kind of chasing around in verbal circles. When asked to define a term, the definer can only define it with a set of words. When asked to define each of these words in turn, he can only do so by defining each by still further sets of words. All these words—and in a usual instance, one would already be involved

[55] *Ibid.*, p. 171.   [56] *Ibid.*, p. 173.
[57] *Ibid.*, pp. 175–177.   [58] *Ibid.*, p. 172.

106

with about sixty words and sixty definitions—must be defined and agreed upon before the discussion can proceed. Even if this were feasible, the argument runs, there would be still another problem. The definer would actually begin to use words he had used before, and so make the whole process circular.[59]

The last important thing Korzybski has to say about definitions is that, due to the impossibility of coming to scientifically exact definitions because of the problem of circularity, it is very necessary to have certain "undefined" terms.[60] Such terms are often "multiordinal" in the sense that they have the adaptability to stand for a great number of objects and for many sets of relationships. They are high on the "abstraction ladder" for this same reason—because they are low in the possession of characteristics but high in the number of real "extensional" things they may be used to refer to. "Structure," "relation," and "nonidentity" are examples of such terms.[61]

We thus see that all linguistic schemes, if analyzed far enough, would depend on a set of undefined terms. If we inquire about the "meaning" of a word, we find that it depends on the "meaning" of other words used in defining it, and that the eventual new relations posited between them ultimately depend *on the m.o. [multiordinal] meanings of the undefined terms,* which, at a given period, cannot be elucidated any further.[62]

Naming, which might be considered as defining in reverse, is considered to be well enough protected, in the General Semantics scheme of things, if the first general principles are observed. If one remembers to avoid the "is" of identity, the "two-valued orientation," "elementalism," and "intensionalism," by consciousness of abstraction, he can name away fairly freely. These four principles are calculated to scare away word magic, ambiguity, and even unfair labelling of people and things.[63]

The completion of the summary of the General Semantics

---

[59] *Ibid.,* pp. 173–175.   [60] Korzybski, *op. cit.,* pp. xxxv–xlii.
[61] *Ibid.,* pp. 433–434.   [62] *Ibid.,* p. 21.
[63] Hayakawa, *Language in Thought and Action,* pp. 187–192.

philosophy of rhetoric brings us to the final discussion in this section: the practical applications of this theory made by Korzybski, Hayakawa, Johnson, and Lee.

THE INSTRUMENTAL APPLICATIONS

Alfred Korzybski invented several devices for the application of his principles to general living. The devices can almost as easily be applied to a teaching rhetoric. One of his frequent complaints was that people sometimes understood his theory but seldom practiced it:

It is not enough to "understand" and "know" the content of the present work; one must *train* oneself in *the use* of the new terms. Then only can he expect the maximum semantic results.[64]

One of the devices to be taught is the limiting of oneself to the kind of terms that are either multiordinal or so basic they cannot be defined. An acquired habit of selecting wherever possible the term that expresses reality as infinite and complex, and continually recognizes the inadequacy of general language to express the wholeness of real events, is Korzybski's desired discipline.[65] There are a number of less important but effective devices used by most General Semanticists. They remind the symbol-user of the facts. "Indexing"[66] appends small numbers to the terms to indicate their scope or sense in a given context; the habit of appending an "etc." to the ends of terms signals their inadequacy to tell the whole story of reality;[67] and the device of segregating terms in quotation marks warns us to check their scope or their differences from other places where they may have been used.[68]

Even Korzybski, of course, expected his theory to be taught practically and estimated that it would not take a long time or be particularly difficult:

[64] Korzybski, *op. cit.*, p. 130.
[65] Korzybski calls this language "nonelementalistic." See Korzybski, *op. cit.*, pp. 32–34.
[66] Hayakawa, *Language in Thought and Action*, p. 214.
[67] Korzybski, *op. cit.*, p. 94.   [68] *Ibid.*, pp. xxxiii–xxxv.

One should not expect this training in General Semantics to be more quickly acquired than the mastering of spelling, or driving a car, or typewriting.[69]

Hayakawa's great contribution, besides bringing the General Semantics theory to education, and providing a clearer interpretation of the general theory, was in the aim of the whole movement. He seems to have conceived it more positively as a way to make people want to cooperate in thought and action:

And what is important for our purposes here is that all this coordination of effort necessary for the functioning of society is *of necessity achieved by language or else it is not achieved at all.*[70]

In criticism of a lot of modern propaganda and advertising, Hayakawa analyzes it as directive language that urges us to do something—vote for some one, buy something, and so on. He points out the harm done when the promises that underlie the directive language are not kept—promises of popularity if one uses some certain brand of cosmetic, for instance. Such broken promises destroy cooperation:

Each of them serves, in greater or less degree, to break down that mutual trust that makes cooperation possible and knits people together into a society.[71]

Mutual cooperation, which seems to come close to being the aim of the art of prose expression in the mind of Hayakawa,[72] has expanding possibilities when it is considered as coming into prominence in an age where so much is decided and accomplished by groups in discussion. It points rather clearly to some new kind of rhetoric that will not so much persuade many to do the single will of one orator, as teach us to be orator and audience by turns with our peers and reach decision and action by the emerging of a residual compromise out of balanced discussion.

[69] *Ibid.*, p. 45.
[70] Hayakawa, *Language in Thought and Action*, p. 18.
[71] *Ibid.*, p. 104.   [72] *Ibid.*, pp. 105–106.

Wendell Johnson also underwrites the theory of Korzybski.[73] But as a professor of speech therapy and psychology, he adds his special application of the General Semantics theory to the prevention and cure of speech disorders in cases of personal adjustment.[74] In *People in Quandaries* (1946), he takes care to point out the important connection between language and personal adjustment:

As a matter of fact, most of the key terms that we customarily use in talking about personality are seen, on close scrutiny, to refer somehow to the reactions that are made to and with words and other symbols.[75]

Johnson provides us with a "schematic stage-by-stage summary of what goes on when Mr. A talks to Mr. B."[76] His diagram (see Figure 7) seems to bring the General Semantics theory to the point where, for his purposes at least, it can be summarized in one schematic view, as Richards managed with his seven instruments of interpretation, and Shannon and Weaver have done with their communication diagram (see page 69). But this is definitely the General Semantics diagram of the communication process. The key difference between this and other diagrams can be indicated by calling attention to the columns on either side of the sound–light waves in the diagram, which represent the non-verbal and the verbal groups of stages. Here again is the central, specifically Korzybskian notion of the abstraction jump between the nonverbal level and the verbal or label level. For Johnson, the important thing is to make the communication process conscious. It involves the kind of language about language that an individual can use upon himself for judging his own language behavior and learning to react healthfully to it:

[73] Wendell Johnson, *People in Quandaries*. Parts II and III of this work are evidently straightforward Korzybskian doctrine. See the Introduction, p. xii.

[74] *Ibid.*, pp. xi–xii.   [75] *Ibid.*, pp. 243–244.   [76] *Ibid.*, p. 472.

1. An event occurs

2. which stimulates Mr. A through eyes, ears, or other sensory organs, and the resulting

3. nervous impulses travel to Mr. A's brain, and from there to his muscles and glands, producing tensions, preverbal "feelings," etc.

4. which Mr. A then begins to translate into words, according to his accustomed verbal patterns, and out of all the words he "thinks of"

5. he "selects," or abstracts, certain ones which he arranges in some fashion, and then

Mr. A speaks to Mr. B

by means of sound waves

and light waves

6. whose ears and eyes are stimulated by the sound waves and light waves, respectively, and the resulting

7. nervous impulses travel to Mr. B's brain, and from there to his muscles and glands, producing tensions, preverbal "feelings," etc.

8. which Mr. B then begins to translate into words, according to *his* accustomed verbal patterns, and out of all the words *he* "thinks of"

9. he "selects," or abstracts certain ones, which he arranges in some fashion and then

Etc. Mr. B speaks, or acts, accordingly, thereby stimulating Mr. A—or somebody else—and so the process of communication goes on, and on—with complications, as indicated . . .

Figure 7—Schematic Stage-by-stage Summary of What Goes on When Mr. A Talks to Mr. B—the Process of Communication. From *People in Quandaries*, by Wendell Johnson (Harper & Brothers, 1946), p. 472. Used by permission.

One can give him a language for talking about his own language—for evaluating his own evaluations. This is done by acquainting him at least with the following . . . .[77]

And at this point Johnson enumerates the more practical devices for forming General Semantics habits.

The terms "inference" and "inferential data" are used by Johnson to refer to the manner in which humans can know scientifically about the atomic and molecular structure of submicroscopic matter, and refer to the inferential findings in this field. We are inferring because we cannot see, but only detect inferentially, the structures in question. Johnson carries this term on to his description of abstraction and uses it to represent the type of abstracting done on all the levels beyond the label level.[78]

This knowledge of what one is doing in one's own language habits, his adjustment to that activity, and his consequent growing ability to communicate it, is the secret of Johnson's application of General Semantics rhetoric to the problems of personal adjustment:

A technique is a way of doing something, and language may be viewed and evaluated as a technique for accomplishing personality adjustment.[79]

. . . . .

With a fair amount of practice one can become reasonably skilled in observing these characteristics of language behavior in oneself and in others. . . . What is involved in these activities determines nothing less than the extent and the limitations of personal development and of social change.[80]

Irving J. Lee's work goes along with Korzybski's theory, too.[81] He has, however, added his own emphasis to one of Korzybski's principles and developed the General Semantics theory in his own field of speech and group discussion.

Lee's "nonallness" principle is an extension of the combined

[77] *Ibid.*, pp. 431–432.   [78] *Ibid.*, pp. 134–136 and 101.
[79] *Ibid.*, p. 269.   [80] *Ibid.*, p. 293.
[81] Lee, *How to Talk with People*, Introduction, pp. xii and xiv.

Korzybskian principles of "organism-as-a-whole" and of "non-identity." It simply warns us that "all," "every," "always," "never," and such absolute terms cannot logically be used because they imply an impossibility—namely, that we can know everything about the event or object we are talking about.[82]

In his special field of speech and discussion, Lee has made careful observations of the phenomena of discussion. Out of these observations he produced *How to Talk with People* (1952), which reduces to fourteen the number of specific problems that clog the progress of free deliberation in discussion groups. For the sake of brevity they can be listed according to their central ideas,[83] and with them the parallel suggestions Lee offers from the General Semantics theory:

1. Misunderstanding because of differences of personal meaning and context of words.
   Suggestion: Don't assume your own meaning; ask the speaker what he means.

2. Contradicting without having enough information.
   Suggestion: Find out in what specific details there is disagreement.

3. Being impatient with any other opinion but one's own.
   Suggestion: Don't try to stop people from having different opinions. Explain for consideration the true process of arriving at suitable compromise through differences.

4. Prescribing for problems rather than describing them.
   Suggestion: The leader must "prod" the group with queries about what the problem is rather than what to do about it.

5. Oversimplifying and classifying problems as old or new, black or white, etc.
   Suggestion: Approach the discussion in case fashion; make no recommendations until the individual case is completely presented.

[82] *Ibid.*, pp. 125–126. Here Lee indicates the limitations of our knowledge as a support for his argument that discussants ought not to be sweeping in their statements.

[83] *Ibid.* The substance of these fourteen problems and their fourteen parallel suggestions is to be found in pages 1–10.

6. Colliding head-on with another disputant because one wants his own way and will not give in an inch to the other.
   Suggestion: Someone should remark on the values of compromise.
7. Name-calling.
   Suggestion: Look beyond the label to the thing.
8. Taking an attack on an idea as a personal attack.
   Suggestion: Neutralize the personal element in one's own or the speaker's words by disclaiming any attempt to seem superior.
9. Getting angry.
   Suggestion: Distract the angry participant by taking a fresh look at the problem from a less disturbing point of view.
10. Monitoring or taking over the discussion (either the leader or any other participant).
    Suggestion: Emphasize the group quality of the work and the nonsolo function of the members.
11. Doing alone what whole committees ought to do (chairman or leader).
    Suggestion: Analyze the agenda and seek cooperation in handling it.
12. Hurrying to inadequate settlements.
    Suggestion: Decide on the time that ought to be spent on the discussion and agree on proportion between the importance of the problem and the time it ought to take.
13. Taking a "business only" attitude and expecting it of everyone else.
    Suggestion: Allow for brief personal deviations in the midst of purposeful business.
14. Taking on too many tasks and responsibilities.
    Suggestion: Arrange for the selection of a participant to handle the job of "reminder" whose function it will be to point out what the chairman or leader cannot keep his attention fixed upon at the moment.

Lee provides here the basis of what promises to become a different kind of rhetoric altogether—a rhetoric of intercommunion instead of persuasion, of talking *with* others instead of talking *at* others:

It dawned on me ever so slowly that it was not enough merely to encourage people to talk *to* others. They needed to know how to talk *with* others too . . . . People need the art of human communion with each other.[84]

Richards and Burke came to this intercommunion also, although not in terms of group discussion techniques. Their communion is an inner parliament within the communicator. Lee is interested in a group as a basis for action.

The completion of the treatment of General Semantics brings us to the end of the summaries of the three emerging philosophies of rhetoric. It remains for us to see the extensions of these theories in Chapter 5 and to examine their possibilities for the improvement of a teaching rhetoric for the first-year classroom.

[84] *Ibid.*, Introduction, p. xi.

Choices and Possibilities for a New Rhetoric

ANALYSIS USUALLY IMPLIES TAKING THINGS APART TO SEE WHAT makes them go. If this is what the examination in the foregoing chapters has done to the theories of Richards, Burke, and the General Semanticists, it will be well to put them together again organically so as to see better their structures and functions as applied to an improved course in teaching rhetoric. No man can make up his mind to buy a car if its parts are spread all along an assembly belt in an automotive plant. But if he goes to the end of the line and examines the finished car carefully, and then gets in and drives it around the block, he can very easily come to a decision. In this part of the study the three theories will be similarly assembled. The points where they meet and the points where they go their separate ways will be considered. The range of choices they offer for a classroom rhetoric will need to be displayed for free appraisal by educators and teachers interested in improving their first-year courses in this field. And finally, since we looked back somewhat carefully as far as Corax and Aristotle, we ought now to be able to look forward. Perhaps we can speculate with profit on the social, cultural, and educational environment of the next ten years of this age of communication, to see how well the three new rhetorics answer the needs of the future.

The present chapter divides naturally into two sections, one providing an outlay of all the choices of elements offered by the three new theories, the other speculating upon the possibilities of the new theories as against the social and cultural demands of the next decade.

CHOICES FOR A NEW RHETORIC

In the first of these two sections, attention must be given to three things: the whole field of choices, the points at which the new theories converge, and the points at which they take their separate ways.

THE WHOLE FIELD OF CHOICES

A complete look at the whole range of choices for a new rhetoric would seem to be best achieved by a chart which would indicate the relative positions of the three new theories in contrast to the positions of the Aristotelian and the current traditional rhetoric. It should also clarify the distinction between a teaching rhetoric and the philosophy of rhetoric. But, above all, it should point out just what changes are advocated by the three new theories.

The chart (pages 118 and 119) has five columns, one for each of the conceptions of rhetoric examined—the Aristotelian conception and its present-day traditional form, and Richards', Burke's, and the General Semanticists' conceptions. The upper section of the chart is devoted to philosophy of rhetoric, while the larger, lower section is given over to "teaching rhetoric" as a course to be used in a first-year classroom. The chart should pro-

	I	II
	ARISTOTLE	**CURRENT TRADITIONAL**

PHILOSOPHY OF RHETORIC

THOUGHT–WORD–
THING RELATIONSHIPS
ABSTRACTION
DEFINITION
LOGIC
DIALECTIC

TEACHING RHETORIC

The "Art" of Rhetoric	GRAMMAR
BOOK I	SYNTAX
Rhetoric	SPELLING
Kinds	PUNCTUATION
Persuasion	MECHANICS
Deliberative	
Forensic	Four Modes of Discourse
Epideictic	Exposition
Deliberative	Description
Orator's Needs	Argumentation
Good	Narration
Happiness	Argumentative
Knowledge	Clarity
Epideictic	Logic
Praise and Blame	Coherence
Virtues	Style Qualities
Amplification	Clearness
Forensic	Force
Law and Wrong	Coherence
Causes of Human Acts	Interest
Justice	Naturalness
Other Means	Other Devices
	Communication
BOOK II	Symbols
	Word Counts
Emotion	Concreteness
The Fourteen Character	Psychology of
Types	Communication
Environments	Audience Reaction, etc.
Topoi	Divisions
Modes of Persuasion	Words
Example	Sentences
Enthememe	Paragraphs
Maxim	The Whole
Concrete Topoi	Specialized Forms
Refutation	Letter
	Essay
BOOK III	Speech
	News
Style	Feature
Clear	Advertising
Natural	T.V. and Radio
Appropriate	Novel
Language	Short Story, etc.
Qualities	
Metaphor	
Simile	
Connotation	
Ambiguity	
Cadence, etc.	
Arrangement	
Divisions, etc.	

A WHOLE-VIEW CHART OF RHETORIC POSSIBILITIES
SHIFT PHILOSOPHIES OF

III	IV	V
RICHARDS	**BURKE**	**GENERAL SEMANTICIST**
THOUGHT–WORD– THING RELATIONSHIPS ABSTRACTION DEFINITION METAPHOR INTERPRETATION INSTRUMENTS	ABSTRACTION DEFINITION DIALECTIC INTERPRETATION MOTIVATION AND IDENTIFICATION PHILOSOPHY OF STYLE	WORD–THING RELATIONSHIPS ABSTRACTION DEFINITION LOGIC DIALECTIC
THOUGHT–WORD– THING RELATIONSHIPS ABSTRACTION DEFINITION METAPHOR INTERPRETATION INSTRUMENTS *(in greater detail)*	ABSTRACTION DEFINITION DIALECTIC INTERPRETATION MOTIVATION AND IDENTIFICATION PHILOSOPHY OF STYLE *(in greater detail)*	WORD–THING RELATIONSHIPS ABSTRACTION DEFINITION LOGIC DIALECTIC *(in greater detail)*
(Next and very secondary) **Some Style Devices but De-emphasized** **Certain Useful Language Information Based Upon "Basic English"**	*(Next all of Aristotle and traditional rhetoric that can be infused with identification)* *The "Art" of Rhetoric* **BOOKS I, II, III** **Useful Parts of Tradi- tional or Current Com- position**	*(Next—very probably—**all** the current **composition** but with emphasis upon Science of Communica- tion)*

vide an oversimplified but clear view of what the three theories are attempting to bring about in a new or improved teaching rhetoric.

Column I gives a very brief sketch of the philosophy of rhetoric taken from sections of Aristotle's works other than the "Rhetorica." Lower in this same column can be seen an outline of what Aristotle built as a teaching rhetoric upon this philosophical basis. Column II provides a composite outline of the elements that time and expediency have added to the teaching rhetoric, now variously called composition, writing, speech, communication, and the like, but still largely Aristotelian in its basic philosophy.

Columns III, IV, and V set up for purposes of comparison the three theories of Richards, Burke, and the General Semanticists. Viewed side by side they display certain common elements. Their philosophies of rhetoric in the upper section of each column seem to have been lifted bodily out of the philosophy section and transplanted into the teaching rhetoric. Nothing could be clearer than that this is actually what Richards is intent upon doing. He has stated that he wants these concerns of his philosophy of rhetoric to take the place of the traditional rhetoric, at least to the extent that the classifying of kinds of devices for hearer–reader effects, usually found in rhetoric texts, should be minimized and squeezed down into the bottom of the lower half of his column, so as to leave room for the "philosophical" concerns that are the real business of rhetoric for him.

That Burke wants to do something similar is also clear. Although he protests that he does not want to do away with the old discipline, and that his philosophical elements are only to be added to it, still these philosophical elements are also expected to pervade the whole of the teaching rhetoric he envisions, because his "identification" has taken over as central term and central aim in place of Aristotle's "persuasion." Burke's philosophy of rhetoric, then, in the upper section of his column, must be fitted into the lower section so as not to disturb the complete *Rhet-*

oric of Aristotle, which is to be found there too, with few changes beyond the substitution of the important central term that colors the whole column.

Putting the General Semanticists into the philosophical section of the chart at all might cause them some embarrassment. After all, they have as many misgivings about the term "philosophy" as Richards has. But it would only be an embarrassment about terms. For they do concern themselves with the same philosophic elements as are found in the other conceptions, and while the term might not suit them well, this study needs a term for the basic elements that will be common to all the theories. Hayakawa and Korzybski certainly intend that such elements be taught in whatever kind of course is to fit young people for a more scientific kind of communication for a more scientific age. So all three theories do actually want to move their "philosophy" of rhetoric down into the lower section of their columns, in order that this philosophy may become a major part of the first-year course in rhetoric.

The reasons why the three newer theories should want to put philosophy, or what we have called philosophy, into English composition and writing courses must be clear from the chapters dealing with each of the theories. The new sciences had given them a new consciousness of the all-pervading importance of language for any study in any field. And language has provided multiple problems never adequately faced before. Having wrestled with these problems in the light of the data from the new sciences, they all seem to have come, by different routes, to the conclusion that the solution of the problems can be begun only by solving the mysteries of abstraction, definition, epistemological relations, metaphor, and motivation. They feel that even freshmen will have to be given what insights are available into these philosophical elements, if they are to raise language to the level of consciousness and reap its richness and efficiency.

Looking back to Aristotle's time, or even to the times of the original trivium and quadrivium, it is likely that the relative simplicity of the curriculum allowed the student of rhetoric to give his whole attention to philosophical concerns like abstraction and logic, definition and epistemology, either immediately before his rhetoric course or simultaneously with it. The consciousness of these basic concerns may well have been strong in students of those days while they composed speeches and themes. But today it is not only quite possible, but quite likely, that the average college student may never make the connection between his philosophy and his composition. In fact, he may go through college without having any course in philosophy at all. Perhaps it is not so surprising that this missing factor, whether one calls it philosophy or not, is being promoted again as a part solution of the problems educators are facing in the field of college composition and communication.

POINTS OF CONCURRENCE IN THE NEW THEORIES

Looking back to earlier chapters, it will be easy to recall several points where all three theories converge. They all agree upon the newly recognized importance of language as the key to man's understanding of himself and his control of his own progress. They agree fairly consistently that it is in his use of language that he functions with his specific nature, that it is language that makes a man human. There is unanimity regarding the first elemental step in abstraction, the lower animal sorting that even humans perform in the unconscious biological reactions. From the general way in which all three theories adopt the gestaltist notion of wholeness and apply it severally to their theories of psychological context, social and economic motivation, or "organism-as-a-whole" attitudes, there seems to be no doubt about the centrality and importance of the new psychologies in the development of a new rhetoric.

Another element in all three theories that is apparent in the three summaries is the emphasis upon the concrete kind of defining as an addition to the genus–species classifications of Aristotle. Definitions in the new theories are attempting to identify things as individuals instead of categorizing them into classifications as in the older philosophies. In the higher levels of abstraction, too, there is almost complete agreement as to the processes of the mind. It is only in some details of the first linguistic or conceptual step in the process that there are differences.

Not only do all three theories agree about the general mental process in the making of metaphors, but they share the credit for drawing attention to the functional as opposed to the decorative importance of metaphor in the fabric of our everyday symbol-using activity. All of them have drawn freely from the newer sciences of sociology, psychology, anthropology, and linguistics, both to inquire into and to support their notions of man's special function as a rhetoric-using animal.

Perhaps, though, the element of deepest unanimity is the end result of all three inquiries. Starting from three different positions—in effect, from Associationism, from mild social cynicism, and from a kind of positivist, anti-Aristotelianism—the Richardsian, Burkeian, and General Semantics theories take three different paths. They are different in method, aims, and background, yet surprisingly enough they all wind up in one place and find one thing they feel should assume prime importance in any new rhetoric—the philosophy of rhetoric.

There are also a few instances where the theories of Richards and Burke converge. Almost the whole of Burke's abstraction theory is as close as possible to that of Richards. Only one relatively unimportant detail concerning the generality of animal perception, which does not really affect the theory of rhetoric to any extent, makes Richards' theory different from that of Aristotle and Burke. They are singularly close in pointing out some of the sources of ambiguity in naming and defining and in their understanding of the emotional and motivational influence upon meaning.

Roots for a New Rhetoric

As we have noted before, not only are the sources and methods of inquiry of the three theories quite dissimilar, but their aims in undertaking the inquiry in the first place and the backgrounds from which they began to work are as disparate as can be. Richards, a linguist and one of the founders of the New Criticism, out of the conservative background of a British university, with little philosophy, but with a great fund of Coleridgean and other literary lore, set himself to find a more efficient interpretation system. Burke, an important literary critic too, but also, by his voluminous reading, a sociologist, psychologist, and humanist, deeply scarred by the social and economic imbalance of his time, decided to explore motives as the true source of deeper meaning. And the General Semanticists, a group enthusiasm, a movement with emotional as well as intellectual conviction, pulled together somehow by the half-angry fire of a Polish-American mathematician and engineer, men representing an iconoclast cause as well as a methodological discipline, aimed their energies at the destruction of traditional logic and epistemology for the sake of the sanity which that destruction would bring to human language relations.

Within the three philosophies of rhetoric, there are many and wide differences. The General Semanticists go their own way in the second level of their abstraction process with a special abstractive step for the jump across the chasm between reality and the realm of the ideal and verbal. Richards and Burke, though they would probably admit the importance of the chasm, would not want to call the spanning of it an act of abstraction.

Epistemologically, there is again no unanimity. Reality, for the General Semanticists, means extensional reality; for Richards it is extensional but includes conceptual realities so long as we give them no special entitive reality. Burke troubles himself with epistemology only enough to show us, by indirection, that his concern with metaphysical notions spells an affinity with Aristotle's metaphysical realism. The General Semanticists protest that there is very little relation, little similarity, between thought and thing. Richards says there is a real relation between them. Burke would very probably hold the older, more traditional conception of thought as the representation of the thing.

Differences in the theory of definition are more like differences in method than in theory. The General Semanticists warn us again and again about the "is" of identity, and about words not being things, while Richards and Burke are offering two methods of identifying, one by finding the referent and the other by a grammatical refining of sentence meaning. They all find quite different reasons why words do not say set things, why they change meaning, why they entangle us in misunderstandings. While agreeing in general on the importance of context in meaning, they disagree as to whether ambiguity comes most of all from an "out-dated" and "two-valued" logic, from a mistaken real relationship between symbols and referents, or from the disparity or shift of the motivational drives of any two persons trying to understand one another.

Richards and Burke really agree upon the importance of purpose, intention, tone, motivation, and the emotive and evaluative factors in language. Their point of comparison is rather a question of emphasis than of contention. Burke builds his theory around motivation. Richards builds his theory around interpretation, of which motivation is one of seven key factors. The General Semanticists would rather not have to worry about keeping the troublesome words that carry ambiguities. They do not, as Burke does, feel that these words have rich advantages, too. They do not even, as Richards does, hope to find a finally efficient system for interpreting them. They think it is wiser not to use such terms at all, but to replace them gradually with what they call "multiordinal" terminology.

The points of comparison within the elements of the three theories are reflected, of course, in the devices they all offer, either for acquiring the language habits that are the implements of the particular theory, or for use in a composition classroom. The devices were invented to fit the theories in question. The seeming resemblance between Richards' and the General Semanticists' system of setting off terms by index numbers and quotation marks almost disappears when one remembers that Richards' device is used largely to distinguish between the diverse functional meanings of a term—feeling, tone, intention, indication—while the General Semanticists' system is used to warn us simply that the term is being used in a certain different sense. Other devices used by all three theories are so diverse in nature and purpose that they need no further comparison.

THE POSSIBILITIES FOR A NEW RHETORIC

A look at the traditional and the newer formulae of rhetoric prompts some hope for a useful synthesis. To give shape to this hope we must first consider what kind of a rhetoric our times call for, and then we must attempt a synthesis suited to the times.

THE ENVIRONMENTAL CHALLENGE TO THE NEW RHETORIC

The fact that social, political, economic, and cultural change have a great influence upon the changing forms of our language arts was one of the basic assumptions in the historical sketch introducing this study. If the *technē* of Corax was created out of a timely urgency to apply rhetoric to the law courts, the eighteenth century tendency to emphasize grammatical correctness grew no less out of an equally important social need to acquire that correctness as the symbol of respectable status.

The cultural needs of the nineteen-sixties will probably determine the shape of the prose expression courses in colleges. Many would say that the needs of any time are the best norm for selection of courses to be used in that time. Certainly it would be safe to say that a course in rhetoric, composition, speech, writing, or communication that did not meet the needs of its time could be put forward only at the risk of failure.

Scholars in many different social and cultural fields of research attest to the fact that the changes occurring today cannot but have deep and lasting effects upon our culture. Pitirim Sorokin, Christopher Dawson, Oswald Spengler, Lewis Mumford, Gilbert Seldes, Harold Innis, Margaret Mead, Arnold Toynbee, and William White are a few of the scholars in various fields who have testified to the vastness and complexity of the changes we are at present undergoing.

There seem to be some significant shifts in process at the present time that have a bearing upon the way we talk to one another.

There are evidences of such significant change in the details of the way ordinary people live. Their relations with their employers have radically changed. They elect committees to discuss their job situations with committees of employment. They state their needs and insist that they be met. They go home from work earlier in the day and earlier in the week than ever before. They live more like their employers. Industries have moved out of the cities to set up in quiet country meadows, and they have taken their workers with them. The whole concept of "going downtown" to shop or see sights or be entertained is changing with the suburban shopping center, the televised transmission of entertainment and sight-seeing. The status-seeking of these ordinary people is bound up with brands of automobiles, vacations in Europe, and being able to afford an analyst. Our grandparents talked proudly of relatives who were schoolteachers. Today our examples of status achieved might as easily be a television star or an industrialist as a college professor who has written a book. All this changing of ways of living and goals of life has to have a profound effect on the motives and meanings behind what we say to one another.

Perhaps we have been affected still more profoundly by the advance of science. Aside from the telling differences that have been made by the avalanche of labor-saving home appliances, the promise of atom-powered transportation, electronic transmission and computation, and a host of other benefits, the exact sciences have provided us with new knowledge that may have an even more lasting influence on our lives. The foundations of our old notions of time and space, density and rarity, solidity and fluidity are crumbling. And in their place we have an invisible and yet unexplained universe of dancing energies structured and restructured in mutations so vast and so swift that we would never notice them even if we could see them.

But the quantum theory in physics and the everbroadening insights of the field theory in psychology have taught us something about this swirl of atoms. The macrocosm of our world in its universe comes more and more to look like the microcosm of the biologist and psychologist. When a microcosm is prodded by a simple stimulus, all the tiniest parts of its structure cooperate in the reaction. When the President of the United States gets a headache the stock market changes. Even when a White House elevator boy gets a headache, the whole world reacts to its effects in some way or other. There is a growing simultaneity to this reaction, too. Effects are felt as quickly, via modern communication, at the far end of the transmission as at the near end. The reaction is instantaneous. Not only is every part of the world affected, but all at the same time, so that everyone can know at once what is going on right now.

The notion of simultaneous reaction to these social and cultural influences brings us to the great revolution in communication today. The social and cultural implications of our huge new systems of intercommunication are so varied and far-reaching that they overwhelm us after a few moments of casual consideration. Television and radio, electronic transmission, the mass distribution of the world's wealth of literature and art, the mass consumption of carloads of printed material that can scarcely pass as art or literature—all this is frightening and yet has possibilities that may conceivably cure its own ills. The simultaneity of the reactions to communication of news, opinions, information, and entertainment demands that young people be trained in critical abilities that will make them aware of and responsible for the means of controlling the mass media.

There is a significant shape also to some of the smaller details of the ways we are beginning to communicate with one another. In government, it is committees that prepare resolutions and get them carried on the Congress floor. In the United Nations the formal speakers are usually doing little more than reporting formally, for the record, what committees have discussed in a rather democratic fashion of dialectical give and take. More conclusions are arrived at nowadays around tables where everyone is on an equal plane than through the older system where a whole audience sat in a block of seats and listened to one speaker. Today the ordinary man seldom gives a formal speech or writes an article. But he does average two or three meetings a week, in which he has responsibility for cooperating with other members of an association in threshing out some problem.

There is another challenge, too, in the growing possibility that advertising may one day completely take over our entertainment. The common man will have to have his critical faculties trained to salvage his recognition of art when Macbeth's dagger is perhaps referred to with the brand name of a cutlery firm.

The challenge that these changes offer is, of course, a challenge to everyone, because it is everyone's language of communication that is involved. But perhaps the first line of defense should be manned by English teachers. Perhaps it is in a good course in prose expression that the ordinary young American ought to find the means to cope with all the threatening but still hopeful chaos the present crisis has brought.

A NEW RHETORIC TO MEET THE CHALLENGE

If one of the needs of the next decade is a new rhetoric to meet this challenge, it will have to answer, point for point, the problems that the challenge creates. Were we to make up a synthetic definition for teaching rhetoric out of all three theories, it would be something like this: the science of recognizing the range of the meanings and of the functions of words, and the art of using and interpreting them in accordance with this recognition. If, in the introduction to this study, we had only a very general definition, now at least we have a more particular one.

Speculating upon the challenge itself might lead to the proposal of at least four requirements for a new rhetoric so defined: it will need to consider its own basic presuppositions as all disciplines must do in a time of crisis and challenge; it will need to broaden its aim until it no longer confines itself to teaching the art of formal persuasion but includes formation in every kind of symbol-using, from a political speech to a kitchen conversation; it will need to adjust itself to the recent studies in the psychology and sociology of communication; and, finally, it will need to make considerable provision for a new kind of speaker–listener situation—the area of group discussion.

We might with profit look at these four elements separately to see how the new rhetoric of the three theories—of Richards, Burke, and the General Semanticists—measures up to the requirements.

We have seen how the three theories asked all the fundamental questions, all the how's and why's about the thought and language problems. There can be little doubt as to the necessity of this philosophy of rhetoric. Sorokin says philosophic inquiry is bound to increase in a time of disintegration like the present:

This means that in times of crisis one should expect an upsurge of cogitation on and study of the how and why, the whence and whither, of man, society, and humanity. This expectation is corroborated by the relevant facts.[1]

[1] Pitirim A. Sorokin, *Social Philosophies of an Age of Crisis* (Boston: The Beacon Press, Inc., 1950), p. 3.

Thus the offerings of the three theories seem to match one of the most important needs of the times.

The projection of a new rhetoric will have to consider the broadening of its aim and scope to include the many other language situations besides that formal and one-to-many situation of the classical orator. It may need to busy itself with the analysis of that rhetoric of the internal forum that an individual uses upon himself when he justifies his own evaluations and manipulates his words to suit the actions his biological, psychological, intellectual, and aesthetic needs demand. If there is a time when adjustment to oneself as well as to one's surroundings becomes a paramount issue, it must be at such a critical time of complex changes as our own. If we all do a great deal more intercommunicating now than ever before, it would seem as though we ought to prepare an art of symbol-using that will cope with all these ways of intercommunicating—listening as well as speaking, reading as well as writing, understanding more efficiently as well as communicating more clearly. We will need instruments of understanding, of interpretation, craft and skill and practical measuring devices for discerning motivation more accurately. Such things are precisely what the three new theories offer in their conceptions of a new rhetoric. The televiewer is the buying public too. If his scrutiny of the public art forms is deepened with Richards' instruments of interpretation, with Burke's pentad format and analysis of literary form, he might know and demand superior entertainment from his advertiser–entertainer. Multiplied by one hundred and fifty million, he alone can tell the advertiser what he wants and get it. It will be this televiewer, trained in this way, who will succeed in controlling the mass media, if anyone does.

The new studies in the psychology and sociology of communication have been examining what happens to the individual and to the social unit when we communicate with one another, especially when we do so in the sharply different ways that the revolution in communication has brought with it. If studies in communication of this sort can be called a specialization of the general philosophy of rhetoric, there can be no doubt that the new teaching rhetoric, with its long, deep foundation in these philosophical matters, will serve as an excellent introduction to the further research that is so critically needed in the fields of psychology and sociology of communication. But whatever their separate duties as college disciplines, communication and rhetoric have much in common, and whichever is taught in the undergraduate curriculum will have to include the essentials of the other. It just happens that from this point of view the new rhetoric will not be found wanting. Its analyses of interpretation and motivation prescribe the same general principles as a good course in communication might begin with. Moreover, Richards and Johnson, at the culminating points in their theories, come to where they can apply their findings most adequately to the very schematic implements that communication scholars use as the basis or outline of their research. The fact that communication, unlike rhetoric or composition or English I, covers the nonverbal kinds of communication need not disturb the community of interest and aim these two disciplines have, nor their efforts to complement rather than hinder one another.

Finally, any rhetoric that looks at the present, let alone the future, will have to make provision for the new kind of discussion rhetoric that is already practiced so universally. The pentad format of Burke, the inquiry process that might serve many purposes as a format for controlling discussion in a democratic manner, but above all the cooperative attitudes of the whole theory of Irving J. Lee and S. I. Hayakawa, provide the beginning, at least, of a specialized section in any new art of rhetoric. If our decision-making process has largely changed to mutual, cooperative discussion that strives for residual compromise, where but in the practical suggestions of Irving Lee could a new discussion rhetoric be better begun?

There have been many other things in the three theories

that were designed explicitly to meet modern needs. Training in
the use of metaphor, philosophy of style, techniques of definition,
and a host of other elements that need no second enumeration,
will meet the modern challenge because they have been created
out of the needs that challenge has already posed.

It should be kept in mind, of course, that the new rhetoric
as viewed in these pages is only a beginning. No one, least of all
the authors of the ideas it involves, would lay claim to more than
that. And among the things that will need examination in the
future studies that deal with it will be the drawing of elaborate
distinctions between rhetoric and dialectic, the examination of
various theories of signs for a deeper grasp of the epistemological
and definitional notions treated so generally here, and possibly—
although pertinent studies are well under way at the present time
—some further research into the psychological problems of audience reaction.

A PROJECTED NEW RHETORIC

Any projected new rhetoric offered by the present writer
must necessarily be limited to one point of view. It must also be
described in a very limited space. And considering such limitations it might be best to name it, describe it by quasi definition,
give a brief outline of its contents, and then describe some areas
more fully to give a hint of the possibilities of the rest.

The concept of rhetoric has been so expanded in the theories of Richards, Burke, and the General Semanticists that it
now includes philosophy of language, the sociology and psychology of communication, and semantics. Its philosophical elements
bring it so close to dialectic that further research is needed to
establish the distinctions between them. The philosophical elements of rhetoric seem also to be the basic elements of its companion arts of grammar and logic. For the new rhetoric, for the
teaching instrument that established all these overlapping relationships, the best label would seem to be "Prose Communication."

Roots for a New Rhetoric

Communication, in the sense of the new rhetoric, is that science and art which provides understanding of the basic presuppositions underlying the functions of discourse, makes use of the findings of literature and science, and teaches the individual how to talk and write, listen and read, in the ways that will suit his needs. The aims here seem clear enough. They include Aristotelian persuasion, and yet they go further to embrace the aim of bringing peace to the individual by showing him how to carry on the discussion of his own inner parliament with himself. Both Richards' and Burke's aims are found here, too, because the student of this kind of a communication course will have to understand the basic notions necessary for good interpretation and effective identification. The scope of the course must be much wider as well as much deeper. It means the kind of communication between speaker and audience, writer and reader, but it also includes the whole range of talking and writing, conversation as well as speeches, office memoranda as well as the historical novel.

As a skeletal outline of the contents of such a course in prose communication, the following may afford at least some notion of the elements, their proportion, emphasis, and location:

PROSE COMMUNICATION

Introduction

The Public Arts and the New Sciences
Literature and Social Expression

Part I: A Philosophy of Communication

Nature and Functions of Language
Words, Thoughts, and Things; Signs and Symbols
The Abstraction Process
Abstraction and Propositions
Abstraction and Verbal Haze
Definition
Ambiguity

Context
Simple, Complex, and Mixed Relations
The Philosophy of Form and Style; Literature
The Interpretation Instruments of I. A. Richards
The Motivation Detection of Kenneth Burke
Some Notions from Philosophers of Language

Part II: A Science of Communication

Psychology of Communication
Sociology of Communication
Related Findings from Biology
Related Findings from Physics
Related Findings from Chemistry
Related Findings from Anthropology
Related Findings from Psychiatry
Related Findings from Linguistics
Various Theories of Signs

Part III: An Art of Communication

Composition
    invention
    organization
    style and metaphor
    literature and communication
Discussion
    attitudes
    compromise
    cooperation
    dialectic residue
    Lee's fourteen suggestions
    leading
    listening
    defining
    scope and circumference
    directional thinking
    Burke's discussion pentad
Conversation
Inner Conversation

Roots for a New Rhetoric

Public Speaking
Professional Writing
   kinds of professional writing
   modes of discourse
Nonverbal Means of Communication

This brief outline indicates the prominence of philosophy and science in the actual teaching rhetoric of such a course in "Prose Communication." Selection has been made, as is evident, from the ideas of Richards and Burke and the General Semanticists, as well as from the ancient ideas of Aristotle.

The introduction to the course might stress the various new uses of communication as observed in public propaganda, advertising, the entertainment industries, psychiatric therapy, discussion situations, and everyday conversation. From this concrete point of departure it would hope to emphasize the pertinent relationships with literature as the communication of accumulated culture.

Part I might embrace the philosophy of rhetoric which has been the central theme of this study and turns out to be more of a revived element than an innovation. It can now be called a philosophy of communication because its elements are basic to far more than the relatively limited scope of the orator's ancient art. Abstraction, definition, and epistemology are foundational to linguistics and grammar, to semantics and logic, in fact to the full sweep of those arts and sciences that relate to the communication of ideas.

Part II could provide the student with the findings of the sciences that pertain to the art of communication, and Part III would introduce rhetoric, in its new broadness of concept, as an art. The new broadness calls for an application of such elements of the three new theories of rhetoric as the aims and resources of each will permit. The outline of the contents shows clearly how much space and emphasis the new rhetoric of discussion must

136

have in a new course that hopes to meet the challenge of the next decade.

Such a course could only be adequately explained in a separate volume. But to provide some idea of how much more fully these headings would be treated, two elements in the outline have been chosen as samples.

The first heading under Part II, A Science of Communication, is Psychology of Communication. This section is intended to acquaint the student with the actual research that has been done up to the present in this field. But it is intended also to make interconnections between the findings of this research and anything else that present science or posterity has provided for our uses. And it so happens that the ancient classifications of audience types listed by Aristotle in the second book of the "Rhetorica"[2] provide the beginnings of a much more detailed classification based upon the findings of psychiatric theory and clinical observation. Aristotle's types may have been fairly vague speculations in his day. But, studied in connection with the modern findings of the pertinent sciences, they promise possibilities in the calculation of audience reaction that are fairly limitless. The immediate course in this projected "Prose Communication" would intend, then, to make a thorough study of what we know today through the psychological sciences, and apply it to the widening and fortifying of Aristotle's types. Such a thorough study would, it seems, provide principles of high probability for the guidance of speakers, writers, and discussion participants in the problems of getting attention and cooperation in their communication activities.

The other element to be treated here, as a sample of the possibilities underlying each of the subheadings, is the topic "scope and circumference" under Discussion in Part III. Recall-

[2] "Rhetorica" in *The Basic Works of Aristotle,* ed. Richard McKeon, trans. Rhys Roberts *et al.* (New York: Random House, Inc., 1941), ii, 12–17, pp. 1403–1408 (1389*a*–1391*b*). Originally published by Oxford University Press, in 1928.

ing Burke's theory of definition and the ambiguities and anti-
monies of definition, the present projected course intends to apply this theory to the processes of group discussion to show its
practicability in such processes. Both the scope and circumference
of an idea and of the symbol that represents it were, in Burke's
theory, indicative of the differences between one individual's idea
of "street" and another's. In the accompanying Figure 8, if A
communicates some information about a "street" to B, he is likely
to transmit to the mind of B very little that belongs to the idea
"street" in his own mind; and at the same time he may be stimulating B to "street" ideas and connotations that are already in B's

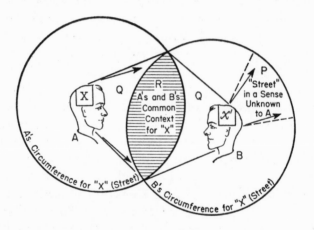

FIGURE 8—CHARTING THE DIRECTION OF DISCUSSION

own receiving mind or memory or nervous system. The point is
that A can be pretty sure that his circumference or context for
the term "street" is different from that of B. He can be pretty
sure also that there are some parts of his "street" context that
are the same as B's. It is in this common area, R, where A and
B are in agreement, or have overlapping contexts about the idea
and term "street," that two minds have the maximum communication efficiency. Maybe, then, what needs to be done is to study

these common areas in communication units and learn how to find them, widen them, and stay within them for purposes of more cooperative discussion.

The process of communication is represented in the accompanying diagram by A communicating idea X with term ✕ to B who receives it as X'. The circles represent the circumferences of A and B for idea X and X'. If, when B is stimulated by A's term ✕, he shoots off on his own contextual tangent, he may be thinking in the direction of sector P, or he might, if the communicator A can manage it, be thinking in sector Q, which is the same as the sector that the communicator A intends. If the two minds meet in this fashion in the common sector, they have come together in that portion of their circumferences where they have common knowledge or experience or more similar contexts. They will be more likely to see eye to eye. Or if they have differences, they will see them more clearly and impartially because they have at least begun to talk about one and the same thing. It is evident how commonly the failure of discussion is due to failure to talk about the same thing. It is also evident that any method for setting the direction of discussion into sectors common to the discussants will be more likely to help them avoid that common discussion failure. Further inspection of this method will only show how the direction can be set by applying Richards' interpretation instruments and Burke's pentad format and the fourteen suggestions of Lee.

Not only does the discussion develop a common ground in this device of sector-aiming, but any discussant or the discussion leader can keep watch over the direction of the discussion at any time by simply listening to the discussants in turn and noting when they select a new sector. If they do, the others must agree to shift their sectors too, so they will have a meeting of minds. Whenever one speaker selects a sector that does not overlap the contexts or circumferences of the other discussants, he is really off the subject until by defining or distinguishing he can provide the others with the information or attitude that will make them possess this sector in common with him.

Such a device for charting the directional activities of discussion needs much more testing and refining. But its application of Burke's definitional theory to the art of group discussion illustrates one interesting use of the new rhetoric theory in a practical circumstance. Such a rhetoric is not limiting or confining. There is ample breadth of choice because, for the more important elements of the new rhetoric, the educator or formulator of a rhetoric has three different approaches to the one new element in Richards, Burke, and the General Semanticists. He can consider the particular requirements of his culture area, philosophy of education, financial limitations, curricular structure, and practical aims, and then choose those elements in the three rhetorics that meet his particular needs.

It is the author's hope, on the completion of this study, that the offerings of I. A. Richards, Kenneth Burke, and the General Semanticists, so seemingly practical and applicable to the solution of English composition curriculum problems, have been made somewhat easier for the individual educator to read and apply to his particular purposes.

Bibliography

BOOKS

ADLER, MORTIMER. *How to Read a Book*. New York: Simon and Schuster, Inc., 1940.

ARISTOTLE. *Aristotle's Psychology*. Translated by WILLIAM A. HAMMOND. New York: The Macmillan Company, 1902.

———. *The "Art" of Rhetoric*. Translated by JOHN H. FREESE. Cambridge, Mass.: Harvard University Press, 1947.

———. *The Basic Works of Aristotle*. Edited by RICHARD MCKEON; translated by RHYS ROBERTS, *et al.* New York: Random House, Inc., 1941.

AYER, ALFRED J. *Language, Truth, and Logic*. New York: Dover Publications, Inc., 1946.

BACON, FRANCIS. "The Great Instauration" and "Novum Organum." *The English Philosophers from Bacon to Mill*, edited by EDWIN A. BURTT. New York: Random House, Inc., 1939.

BALDWIN, CHARLES S. *Ancient Rhetoric and Poetic*. New York: The Macmillan Company, 1924.

———. *Medieval Rhetoric and Poetic*. New York: The Macmillan Company, 1928.

BARRETT, E. BOYD. *Motive-Force and Motivation-Tracks*. New York: Longmans, Green & Company, Inc., 1911.

BEESLEY, PATRICIA. *The Revival of the Humanities in American Education*. New York: Columbia University Press, 1940.

141

Bibliography

BERGSON, HENRI. *Creative Evolution.* New York: Henry Holt & Co., Inc., 1911.

————. *The Creative Mind: An Introduction to Metaphysics.* Translated by MABELLE ANDISON. New York: Philosophical Library, Inc., 1946.

BLACK, MAX. *Critical Thinking: An Introduction to Logic and the Scientific Method.* Englewood Cliffs, N.J.: Prentice-Hall, Inc., 1946.

————. *Language and Philosophy.* Ithaca, N.Y.: Cornell University Press, 1949.

BLAIR, HUGH. *An Abridgement of Lectures on Rhetoric.* Philadelphia: Key, Meilke, and Biddle, 1832.

BLOOMFIELD, LEONARD. *Language.* New York: Henry Holt & Co., Inc., 1933.

BOAS, FRANZ. *Race, Language, and Culture.* New York: The Macmillan Company, 1940.

————. *The Mind of Primitive Man.* New York: The Macmillan Company, 1938.

BONNER, ROBERT J. *Lawyers and Litigants in Ancient Athens.* Chicago: University of Chicago Press, 1927.

BREASTED, JAMES H., and ROBINSON, JAMES H. *History of Europe: Ancient and Medieval.* Boston: Ginn & Company, 1920.

BRITTON, KARL. *John Stuart Mill.* London: Penguin Books, Ltd., 1953.

BRYSON, LYMAN (ed.). *The Communication of Ideas.* New York: Harper & Brothers, 1948.

BURKE, KENNETH. *Counter-Statement,* 2nd ed., rev., Los Altos, Calif.: Hermes Publications, 1953.

————. *A Grammar of Motives.* Englewood Cliffs, N.J.: Prentice-Hall, Inc., 1945.

————. *Permanence and Change,* 2nd ed., rev., Los Altos, Calif.: Hermes Publications, 1954.

————. *The Philosophy of Literary Form.* Baton Rouge, La.: Louisiana State University Press, 1941.

————. *A Rhetoric of Motives.* New York: George Braziller, Inc., c1950.

————. *Towards a Better Life*. New York: Harcourt, Brace, & Co., 1932.

BURTT, EDWIN A. (ed.). *The English Philosophers from Bacon to Mill*. New York: Random House, Inc., 1939.

BUTCHER, S. H. *Some Aspects of Greek Genius*. London: Macmillan & Co., Ltd., 1893.

CAHILL, E. *The Framework of a Christian State*. Dublin: M. H. Gill & Son, Ltd., 1932.

CAMPBELL, GEORGE. *The Philosophy of Rhetoric*. Boston: J. H. Wilkins & Co., Hilliard, Gray, and Co., and Gould, Lincoln, and Kendall, 1835.

CASSIRER, ERNST. *Language and Myth*. Translated by SUSANNE K. LANGER. New York: Doubleday Anchor Books, Inc., 1953.

CHASE, STUART. *The Power of Words*. New York: Harcourt, Brace & Co., 1954.

CICERO. *De Oratore*. Edited by A. S. WILKINS. 3 vols. 3rd ed. London: The Clarendon Press, 1893.

CICERONIS, M. TULLI. *De Oratore*. Edited by E. P. Crowell. Philadelphia: Eldredge & Brother, 1879.

CLARK, DONALD L. *Rhetoric in Greco-Roman Education*. New York: Columbia University Press, 1957.

COFFEY, P. *Epistemology: or the Theory of Knowledge*. 2 vols. Gloucester, Mass.: Peter Smith, 1938.

COON, CARLETON S. *The Story of Man*. New York: Alfred A. Knopf, Inc., 1954.

CRANE, R. S. (ed.). *Critics and Criticism*. Chicago: University of Chicago Press, 1952.

CROCE, BENEDETTO. *Politics and Morals*. Translated by SALVATORE J. CASTIGLIONE. New York: Philosophical Library, Inc., 1945.

DANTE. *De Vulgari Eloquentia*. Translated by A. G. F. HOWELL. London: J. M. Dent & Sons, Ltd., 1904.

DAWSON, CHRISTOPHER. *Religion and Culture*. New York: Sheed & Ward, 1948.

DEWEY, JOHN. *Intelligence and the Modern World*. Edited by JOSEPH RATNER. New York: Random House, Inc., 1939.

————. *Logic, The Theory of Inquiry*. New York: Henry Holt and Co., Inc., 1938.

————, and BENTLEY, ARTHUR. *Knowing and the Known.* Boston: Beacon Press, Inc., 1949.

DIONYSIUS OF HALICARNASSUS. *On Literary Composition.* Translated by RHYS ROBERTS. London: Macmillan and Co., Ltd., 1910.

DONNELLY, F. P. *Art Principles in Literature.* New York: The Macmillan Company, 1923.

————. *Literary Art and Modern Education.* New York: P. J. Kenedy & Sons, 1927.

DUFF, J. WIGHT. *A Literary History of Rome in the Silver Age.* New York: Charles Scribner's Sons, 1927.

EMPSON, WILLIAM. *Seven Types of Ambiguity.* New York: Meridian Books, Inc., 1955.

ERGANG, ROBERT. *Europe: From the Renaissance to Waterloo.* Boston: D. C. Heath & Company, 1939.

EYSENCK, H. J. *Uses and Abuses of Psychology.* London: Penguin Books, Ltd., 1953.

FLEMING, T. V. *Foundations of Philosophy.* London: The Shakespeare Head Press, 1949.

FORDHAM, FRIEDA. *An Introduction to Jung's Psychology.* London: Penguin Books, Ltd., 1953.

FRÖBES, JOSEPH. *Compendium Psychologiae Experimentalis.* Rome: Gregorian University Press, 1937.

GENY, PAUL. *Critica: De Cognitionis Humanae Valore Disquisitio,* 3rd ed. Rome: Gregorian University Press, 1932.

GILBERT, ALLAN H. *Literary Criticism: Plato to Dryden.* New York: American Book Company, 1940.

GILSON, ETIENNE. *History of Christian Philosophy in the Middle Ages.* New York: Random House, Inc., 1955.

GRAY, GILES W., and WISE, CLAUDE M. *The Bases of Speech,* 2nd ed., rev., New York: Harper & Brothers, 1946.

GREEN, JOHN R. *A Short History of the English People,* 2nd ed., rev., New York: Harper & Brothers, 1899.

HAARHOFF, THEODORE. *Schools of Gaul: A Study of Pagan and Christian Education in the Last Century of the Western Empire.* London: Oxford University Press, 1920.

HAYAKAWA, S. I. *Language in Thought and Action.* New York: Harcourt, Brace & Co., 1949.

———— (ed.). *Language, Meaning and Maturity.* New York: Harper & Brothers, 1954.

HIGHET, GILBERT. *Man's Unconquerable Mind.* New York: Columbia University Press, 1954.

HOLLINGWORTH, H. L. *The Psychology of Thought.* New York: Appleton-Century-Crofts, Inc., 1927.

HORACE. *Ars Poetica.* Translated by T. A. MOXON. London: J. M. Dent & Sons, Ltd., 1941.

HORATII. *Opera Omnia Horatii.* Edited by A. J. MACLEANE. London: George Bell & Sons, Ltd., 1953.

HOWELL, WILBUR S. *Logic and Rhetoric in England: 1500–1700.* Princeton, N.J.: Princeton University Press, 1956.

HYMAN, STANLEY E. *The Armed Vision.* New York: Vintage Books, Inc., 1955.

ISOCRATES. *Logoi Tessereskaideka.* Edited by WILLIAM BATTIE. London: C. Davis, J. Whiston, and B. Dod, 1748.

JAEGER, WERNER. *Aristotle.* Translated by RICHARD ROBINSON. London: The Clarendon Press, 1934.

————. *Paideia: The Ideals of Greek Culture.* Translated by GILBERT HIGHET. New York: Oxford University Press, Vol. I, 1945; Vol. II, 1943; Vol. III, 1944.

JAMES, WILLIAM. *Pragmatism.* New York: Longmans, Green & Co., Inc., 1928.

————. *The Principles of Psychology.* New York: Henry Holt & Co., Inc., 1918.

————. *Psychology.* New York: Henry Holt & Co., Inc., 1892.

JEBB, R. C. (ed.). *Selections from the Attic Orators,* 2nd ed., rev. London: Macmillan and Co., Ltd., 1927.

JESPERSON, OTTO H. *The Philosophy of Grammar.* New York: Henry Holt & Co., Inc., 1924.

JEVONS, FRANK B. *A History of Greek Literature.* London: Charles Griffin and Co., Ltd., 1886.

JOHNSON, WENDELL. *People in Quandaries.* New York: Harper & Brothers, 1946.

KANT, EMMANUEL. *Critique of Practical Reason.* Translated by T. K. ABBOTT. 6th ed. London: Longmans, Green & Co., Ltd., 1927.

Bibliography

KITZHABER, ALBERT R. *A Bibliography on Rhetoric in American Colleges: 1850–1900.* Denver: Bibliographical Center for Research, Denver Public Library, 1954.

KNIGHT, MARGARET (ed.). *William James: A Selection from His Writings on Psychology.* London: Penguin Books, Ltd., 1950.

KOFFKA, KURT. *The Growth of the Mind.* Translated by R. M. OGDEN. London: Routledge & Kegan Paul, Ltd., 1924.

————. *The Principles of Gestalt Psychology.* New York: Harcourt, Brace & Co., 1935.

KOHLER, WOLFGANG. *Gestalt Psychology.* New York: Horace Liveright, 1929.

KORZYBSKI, ALFRED. *Science and Sanity,* 3rd ed., rev. Lakeville, Conn.: The International Non-Aristotelian Library Publishing Co., 1948.

LANGER, SUSANNE K. *Philosophy in a New Key.* Cambridge, Mass.: Harvard University Press, 1951.

LASKI, HAROLD. *Reflections on the Revolution of Our Time.* New York: The Viking Press, Inc., 1943.

LASSWELL, HAROLD D. *Democracy Through Public Opinion.* Menasha, Wis.: George Banta Publishing Company, 1941.

————. *Propaganda Technique in the World War.* New York: Alfred A. Knopf, Inc., 1927.

LAZARSFELD, PAUL F. *Communication Research.* New York: Harper & Brothers, 1949.

LEE, IRVING J. *How to Talk with People.* New York: Harper & Brothers, 1952.

————. *Language Habits in Human Affairs.* New York: Harper & Brothers, 1941.

————, (ed.). *The Language of Wisdom and Folly.* New York: Harper & Brothers, 1949.

LERNER, MAX. *Ideas Are Weapons.* New York: The Viking Press, Inc., 1939.

LINTON, RALPH. *The Cultural Background of Personality.* New York: Appleton-Century-Crofts, Inc., 1945.

————. *The Tree of Culture.* New York: Alfred A. Knopf, Inc., 1955.

LIPPMANN, WALTER. *Public Opinion.* New York: Harcourt, Brace & Co., 1922.

LIVINGSTONE, R. W. *The Greek Genius and Its Meaning to Us.* 2nd ed. London: The Clarendon Press, 1915.

LONGINUS, CASSIUS. *Commentarius de Sublimitate Dionysii.* Revised by ZACHARIO PEARCE. New York: Ebenezer F. Backus, 1812.

LORGE, IRVING, and THORNDIKE, EDWARD L. *A Semantic Count of English Words.* New York: Bureau of Publications, Teachers College, Columbia University, 1938.

MAHAFFY, J. P. *A History of Classical Greek Literature.* 2 vols. 2nd ed., rev. London: Longmans, Green & Co., Ltd., 1883.

————. *Social Life in Greece.* London: Macmillan & Co., Ltd., 1888.

————. *A Survey of Greek Civilization.* Meadville, Pa.: The Century Press, 1896.

MALINOWSKI, BRONISLAW. *Magic, Science, and Religion and Other Essays.* New York: Doubleday Anchor Books, Inc., 1954.

MANNHEIM, KARL. *Ideology and Utopia: An Introduction to the Sociology of Knowledge.* Translated by LOUIS WIRTH and EDWARD SILS. New York: The International Library of Psychology, Philosophy, and Scientific Method, 1936.

MARITAIN, JACQUES. *Bergsonian Philosophy and Thomism.* Translated by MABELLE and GORDON ANDISON. New York: Philosophical Library, Inc., 1955.

————. *The Degrees of Knowledge.* New York: Charles Scribner's Sons, 1938.

McGRATH, EARL J. (ed.). *Communication in General Education.* Dubuque, Iowa: William C. Brown Company, 1949.

McKILLOP, ANNE SELLEY. *The Relationship Between the Reader's Attitude and Certain Types of Reading Response.* New York: Bureau of Publications, Teachers College, Columbia University, 1952.

MEAD, GEORGE H. *Mind, Self, and Society.* Chicago: University of Chicago Press, 1943.

MEAD, MARGARET. *New Lives for Old.* New York: William Morrow & Co., Inc., 1956.

MENCKEN, H. L. *The American Language.* New York: Alfred A. Knopf, Inc., 1931.

147

Bibliography

MESTRE, PÈRE. *Préceptes de Rhétorique: Histoire de l'Eloquence Grecque, Latine, et Française.* 7th ed. Lyon: Delhomme et Brignet, 1893.

MILL, JOHN S. *The Philosophy of Scientific Method.* Edited by ERNEST NAGEL. New York: Hafner Publishing Co., Inc., 1950.

MOREY, WILLIAM C. *Outlines of Greek History.* New York: American Book Company, 1908.

MORRIS, CHARLES. *Signs, Language, and Behavior.* New York: George Braziller, Inc., 1955.

MOTT, FRANK. *Golden Multitudes.* New York: The Macmillan Company, 1947.

O'BRIEN, ARTHUR. *Europe before Modern Times.* Chicago: Loyola University Press, 1940.

OGDEN, C. K., and RICHARDS, I. A. *The Meaning of Meaning.* London: Routledge and Kegan Paul, Ltd., 1923.

OSBORN, ALEXANDER F. *Applied Imagination: Principles and Procedures of Creative Thinking.* 2nd ed., rev. New York: Charles Scribner's Sons, 1957.

PEI, MARIO. *The Story of Language.* New York: J. B. Lippincott Co., 1949.

PEIRCE, CHARLES S. *Philosophical Writings of Peirce.* 2nd ed. rev. Edited by JUSTUS BUCHLER. New York: Dover Publications, Inc., 1955.

PIAGET, JEAN. *The Language and Thought of the Child.* New York: Meridian Books, Inc., 1955.

PLATO. *The Dialogues of Plato.* 2 vols. 3rd ed. Translated by B. JOWETT. New York: Random House, Inc., 1937.

————. *The Works of Plato.* 3rd ed. Edited by IRWIN EDMAN and translated by B. JOWETT. New York: Simon and Schuster, Inc., 1928.

POLLOCK, THOMAS C. *The Nature of Literature: Its Relation to Science, Language, and Human Experience.* Princeton, N.J.: Princeton University Press, 1942.

POTTER, SIMEON. *Our Language.* Harmondsworth, Middlesex, England: Penguin Books, Ltd., 1951.

QUILLER-COUCH, ARTHUR. *On the Art of Writing.* Cambridge, England: Cambridge University Press, 1946.

QUINTILIANUS. *Institutio Oratoria.* 4 vols. Translated by H. E. BUTLER. Cambridge, Mass.: Harvard University Press, 1953.

Ratio atque Institutio Studiorum Societatis Jesu. Woodstock, Md.: Woodstock College Press, 1932.

RICHARDS, I. A. *Basic English and Its Uses.* New York: W. W. Norton & Company, Inc., 1943.

————. *Coleridge on Imagination.* London: Kegan Paul, Trench, Trubner, and Co., Ltd., 1934.

————. *How to Read a Page.* New York: W. W. Norton & Company, Inc., 1942.

————. *Interpretation in Teaching.* New York: Harcourt, Brace & Co., c1938.

————. *Mencius on the Mind.* New York: Harcourt, Brace & Co., 1932.

————. *The Philosophy of Rhetoric.* New York: Oxford University Press, c1936.

————. *Practical Criticism.* New York: Harcourt, Brace & Co., c1929.

————. *Principles of Literary Criticism.* London: Routledge and Kegan Paul, Ltd., c1924.

————. *Speculative Instruments.* Chicago: University of Chicago Press, 1955.

RUSSELL, BERTRAND. *Human Knowledge, Its Scope and Limits.* New York: Simon and Schuster, Inc., 1948.

SANDYS, JOHN E. (ed.). *A Companion to Latin Studies.* 3rd ed., rev. London: Cambridge University Press, 1935.

SAPIR, EDWARD. *Culture, Language, and Personality: Selected Essays.* Edited by DAVID G. MANDELBAUM. Los Angeles: University of California Press, 1956.

————. *Language: An Introduction to the Study of Speech.* New York: Harcourt, Brace & Co., 1921.

SCHLAUCH, MARGARET. *The Gift of Language.* New York: Dover Publications, Inc., 1955.

SCHRAMM, WILBUR. *Communication in Modern Society.* Urbana, Ill.: University of Illinois Press, 1948.

————. *Mass Communication.* Urbana, Ill.: University of Illinois Press, 1949.

Bibliography

SCHUTZ, MARTIN. *Academic Illusions*. Chicago: University of Chicago Press, 1933.

SELDES, GILBERT. *The Great Audience*. New York: The Viking Press, Inc., 1950.

SHANNON, CLAUDE E., and WEAVER, WARREN. *The Mathematical Theory of Communication*. Urbana, Ill.: University of Illinois Press, 1949.

SHERMAN, MANDEL. *Basic Problems of Behavior*. New York: Longmans, Green & Co., Inc., 1941.

SHOEMAKER, FRANCIS. *Aesthetic Experience and the Humanities*. New York: Columbia University Press, 1943.

SOROKIN, PITIRIM A. *Social and Cultural Dynamics*. 2 vols. New York: American Book Company, 1937.

————. *Social Philosophies of an Age of Crisis*. Boston: The Beacon Press, Inc., 1950.

————. *Society, Culture, and Personality: Their Structure and Dynamics*. New York: Harper & Brothers, c1947.

SPENCER, HERBERT. *Philosophy of Style*. Boston: Allyn & Bacon, Inc., 1892.

STOCKS, J. L. *Aristotelianism*. Boston: Marshall Jones Co., 1925.

STRECKER, EDWARD A. *Basic Psychiatry*. New York: Random House, Inc., 1952.

TACITUS, P. CORNELIUS. *Dialogus de Oratoribus*. Edited by ALFRED GUDEMAN. Boston: Ginn & Company, 1894.

TAYLOR, A. E. *Aristotle*. 2nd ed., rev. New York: Dover Publications, Inc., 1955.

THONSSEN, LESTER, and BAIRD, A. CRAIG. *Speech Criticism*. New York: The Ronald Press Company, 1948.

THUCYDIDES. *The Complete Writings of Thucydides*. Translated by P. CRAWLEY. New York: Random House, Inc., 1951.

TIMASHEFF, NICHOLAS F. *Sociological Theory: Its Nature and Growth*. Garden City, N.Y.: Doubleday & Company, Inc., 1955.

TINDALL, WILLIAM Y. *Forces in Modern British Literature: 1885–1956*. New York: Vintage Books, Inc., 1956.

TOYNBEE, ARNOLD J. *A Study of History*. Abridgements of Volumes I–IV by D. C. SOMERVELL. New York: Oxford University Press, 1947.

TRILLING, LIONEL. *The Opposing Self.* New York: The Viking Press, Inc., 1955.

THORNDIKE, EDWARD L. *Psychology of Wants, Interests, and Attitudes.* New York: Appleton-Century-Crofts, Inc., 1935.

UTTERBACK, WILLIAM E. *Group Thinking and Conference Leadership.* New York: Rinehart & Company, Inc., 1950.

VEBLEN, THORSTEIN. *The Theory of the Leisure Class.* New York: The Viking Press, Inc., 1924.

WALPOLE, HUGH. *Semantics: The Nature of Words and Their Meaning.* New York: W. W. Norton & Company, Inc., 1941.

WATSON, J. B. *Psychology from the Standpoint of the Behaviorist.* 3rd ed., rev. Philadelphia: J. B. Lippincott Co., 1929.

WEAVER, RICHARD M. *The Ethics of Rhetoric.* Chicago: Henry Regnery Co., 1953.

WHIBLEY, LEONARD (ed.). *A Companion to Greek Studies.* 4th ed., rev. London: Cambridge University Press, 1931.

WHITE, LLEWELLYN, and LEIGH, ROBERT D. *Peoples Speaking to Peoples.* Chicago: University of Chicago Press, 1946.

WHITEHEAD, ALFRED N. *Science and the Modern World.* New York: The Macmillan Company, 1925.

WIENER, NORBERT. *Cybernetics: or Control and Communication in the Animal and the Machine.* New York: John Wiley & Sons, Inc., 1948.

———. *The Human Use of Human Beings: Cybernetics and Society.* Boston: Houghton Mifflin Company, 1950.

WITTGENSTEIN, LUDWIG. *Philosophical Investigations.* New York: The Macmillan Company, 1953.

WOODWORTH, ROBERT S. *Experimental Psychology.* New York: Henry Holt & Co., Inc., 1938.

WRIGHT, WILMER C. *A Short History of Greek Literature.* New York: American Book Company, 1907.

ZIMMERN, ALFRED. *The Greek Commonwealth: Politics and Economics in Fifth-Century Athens.* 2nd ed., rev. London: Oxford University Press, 1952.

ZIPF, G. K. *The Psychology of Language.* Boston: Houghton Mifflin Company, 1935.

Bibliography

ARTICLES

ALY, BOWER. "The Rhetoric of Semantics," *The Quarterly Journal of Speech*, XXX (February, 1944), pp. 23–30.

————. "The Scientist's Debt to Rhetoric," *The Quarterly Journal of Speech*, XXII (December, 1936), pp. 584–590.

ANDERSON, JEANETTE. "A Critique of General Semantics: Two Times Two Is the Same for Everybody, But One Never Is." *The Quarterly Journal of Speech*, XXIX (April, 1943), pp. 187–195.

BARZUN, JACQUES. "Scientific Humanism," *The Nation*, CXLVIII (April, 1939), pp. 502–503.

BRYANT, DONALD C. "Aspects of Rhetorical Tradition: The Intellectual Foundation," *The Quarterly Journal of Speech*, XXXVI (April, 1950 and October, 1950), pp. 169–176 and 326–332.

————. "Rhetoric: Its Function and Scope," *The Quarterly Journal of Speech*, XXXIX (December, 1953), pp. 401–424.

————. "Some Problems of Scope and Method in Rhetorical Scholarship," *The Quarterly Journal of Speech*, XXIII (April, 1937), pp. 182–189.

BURKE, KENNETH. "A Dramatistic View of the Origins of Language," *The Quarterly Journal of Speech*, Part I, XXXVIII (October, 1952), pp. 251–264; Part II, XXXVIII (December, 1952), pp. 446–460; Part III, XXXIX (February, 1953), pp. 79–92.

————. "Ethan Brand: A Preparatory Investigation," *The Hopkins Review*, V (Winter, 1952), pp. 45–46.

————. "Fact, Inference, and Proof in the Analysis of Literary Symbolism," in *Symbols and Values: An Initial Study*, edited by Lyman Bryson, Louis Finkelstein, R. M. MacIver, and Richard McKeon. New York: Harper & Brothers, 1954, pp. 283–287.

————. "Postscripts on the Negative," *The Quarterly Journal of Speech*, XXXIX (October, 1953), pp. 209–216.

————. "Progress: Promise and Problems," *The Nation*, Vol. 185, No. 15 (April 13, 1957), pp. 322–324.

————. "Rhetoric Old and New," *The Journal of General Education*, V (April, 1951), pp. 203–205.

152

————. "Symbol and Association," *The Hudson Review*, IX, No. 2 (Summer, 1956), pp. 212–225.

CLARK, DONALD L. "Literature and Science," *MS. A Magazine for Writers*, III (April, 1932), pp. 1–9.

————. "The Place of Rhetoric in a Liberal Education," *The Quarterly Journal of Speech*, XXXVI (October, 1950), pp. 291–295.

CROCKER, LIONEL. "Rhetoric in the Beginning Course," *The Quarterly Journal of Speech*, XXIX (October, 1943), pp. 314–317.

DE LAGUNA, GRACE A. "Communication: The Act, and the Object with Reference to Mead," *The Journal of Philosophy*, XLIII (April, 1946), pp. 225–238.

EHNINGER, DOUGLAS. "A Logic of Discussion Method," *The Quarterly Journal of Speech*, XXIX (April, 1943), pp. 163–167.

GREY, LENNOX. "Test Case," *Teachers College Record*, LVII (November, 1955), pp. 129–138.

HABERMAN, FREDERICK W. (ed.). "A Bibliography of Rhetoric and Public Address for the Year 1948," *The Quarterly Journal of Speech*, XXXV (April, 1949), pp. 127–148.

————. "A Bibliography of Rhetoric and Public Address for the Year 1949," *The Quarterly Journal of Speech*, XXXVI (April, 1950), pp. 141–163.

HOCHMUTH, MARIE. "Kenneth Burke and the 'New' Rhetoric," *The Quarterly Journal of Speech*, XXXVIII (April, 1952), pp. 133–144.

HOLLAND, LAURA V. "Kenneth Burke's Dramatistic Approach to Speech Criticism," *The Quarterly Journal of Speech*, XLI (December, 1955), pp. 352–358.

————. "Rhetorical Criticism: A Burkeian Method," *The Quarterly Journal of Speech*, XXXIX (December, 1953), pp. 444–450.

HUNT, EVERETT L. "Rhetoric and General Education," *The Quarterly Journal of Speech*, XXXV (October, 1949), pp. 275–283.

JEBB, R. C. "Rhetoric," *Encyclopaedia Britannica*, XIX (1954), pp. 247–248.

KILPATRICK, F. P. "Perception Theory and General Semantics," *ETC: A Review of General Semantics*, XVII (Summer, 1955), pp. 257–264.

Bibliography

LEE, IRVING J. "General Semantics and Public Speaking," *The Quarterly Journal of Speech*, XXVI (December, 1940), pp. 594–606.

————. "General Semantics: 1952," *The Quarterly Journal of Speech*, XXXVIII (February, 1952), pp. 1–22.

McKEON, RICHARD. "The Nature and Teaching of the Humanities," *The Journal of General Education*, III (July, 1949), pp. 290–303.

MORRIS, CHARLES. "The Teaching of Oral and Written Communication as a United Program of Language Instruction," *The Quarterly Journal of Speech*, XXIX (April, 1943), pp. 209–212.

MURRAY, ELWOOD. "The Semantics of Rhetoric," *The Quarterly Journal of Speech*, XXX (February, 1944), pp. 31–41.

NATANSON, MAURICE. "The Limits of Rhetoric," *The Quarterly Journal of Speech*, XLI (April, 1955), pp. 133–139.

NEWMAN, JOHN B. "The Area of Semantics," *The Quarterly Journal of Speech*, XLIII (April, 1957), pp. 155–164.

NORTH, HELEN F. "Rhetoric and Historiography," *The Quarterly Journal of Speech*, XLII (October, 1956), pp. 234–242.

PARRISH, W. M. "The Tradition of Rhetoric," *The Quarterly Journal of Speech*, XXXIII (December, 1947), pp. 465–467.

"Rhetorica ad Herennium," A translation of Book I by RAY NADEAU, *Speech Monographs*, XVI (August, 1949), pp. 57–68.

"Rhetoric and General Education: A Symposium," *The Quarterly Journal of Speech*, XXXV (December, 1949), pp. 419–426, and XXXVI (February, 1950), pp. 1–9.

SAMS, HENRY W. "Composition and Logic," *The Journal of General Education*, VI (July, 1952), pp. 268–279.

SATTLER, WILLIAM M. "Socratic Dialect and Modern Group Discussion," *The Quarterly Journal of Speech*, XXIX (April, 1943), pp. 152–157.

SHOEMAKER, FRANCIS. "Communication and Community Life," *The English Journal*, XXXVI (November, 1947), pp. 459–464.

TARSKI, ALFRED. "The Semantic Conception of Truth and the Foundation of Semantics," in *Semantics and the Philosophy of Language*, edited by Leonard Linsky. Urbana, Ill.: University of Illinois Press, 1952.

THONSSEN, LESTER. "Recent Literature in Rhetoric," *The Quarterly Journal of Speech,* XXXIX (December, 1953), pp. 501–505.

UTTERBACK, WILLIAM E. "Independent Variables in the Conference Situation," *The Quarterly Journal of Speech,* XL (December, 1954), pp. 381–387.

WALLACE, KARL R. "Aspects of Modern Rhetoric in Francis Bacon," *The Quarterly Journal of Speech,* XLII (December, 1956), pp. 398–406.

WILEY, EARL W. "Rhetoric in Beginning Courses," *The Quarterly Journal of Speech,* XXIX (October, 1943), pp. 314–317.

———. "The Rhetoric of American Democracy," *The Quarterly Journal of Speech,* XXIX (April, 1943), pp. 157–163.

UNPUBLISHED SOURCES

Andover, New Jersey, Kenneth Burke's typewritten notes on the first draft of this study. September 24, 1956; December 22, 1956; and January 3, 1957.

Andover, New Jersey, Personal interview with Kenneth Burke, January 3, 1957.

Cambridge, Massachusetts, I. A. Richards' notes on the first draft of this study, with an accompanying letter. December 7, 1956.

Cambridge, Massachusetts, Personal interview with I. A. Richards, October 5, 1956.

FORSDALE, LOUIS. "The Interdivisional Program in Communication and the Communication Arts at Teachers College," Unpublished Doctor's project, Teachers College, Columbia University, 1951.

HARDY, WILLIAM G. "Some Semantic Theories," Unpublished Ph.D. dissertation, Cornell University, 1943.

HOLLAND, LAURA V. "Aristotelianism in the Rhetorical Theory of Kenneth Burke," Unpublished Ph.D. dissertation, University of Illinois, 1955.

KNOX, GEORGE A. "Kenneth Burke as Literary Theorist and Critic," Unpublished Ph.D. dissertation, University of Washington, 1953.

New York, Personal interviews with Kenneth Burke, September 24, 1956; and May 29, 1957.

Bibliography

New York, Personal interview with S. I. Hayakawa, May 28, 1957.

PENCE, ORVILLE L. "The Concept and Function of Logical Proof in the Rhetorical System of Richard Whateley," Unpublished Ph.D. dissertation, University of Iowa, 1947.

TEXTBOOKS

APP, AUSTIN J. *The Way to Creative Writing.* Milwaukee: Bruce Publishing Co., 1954.

BORCHERS, GLADYS L. *Living Speech.* New York: Harcourt, Brace & Co., 1946.

———— and WISE, CLAUDE M. *Modern Speech.* New York: Harcourt, Brace & Co., 1947.

BROOKS, CLEANTH, and WARREN, ROBERT P. *Modern Rhetoric with Readings.* New York: Harcourt, Brace & Co., 1950.

CALLAN, FRANK H. *Excellence in English.* New York: The Devin-Adair Co., 1924.

CANBY, HENRY S., et al. *English Composition in Theory and Practice.* New York: The Macmillan Company, 1933.

CARGILL, OSCAR, et al. *New Highways in College Composition.* 2nd ed. Englewood Cliffs, N.J.: Prentice-Hall, Inc., 1955.

DEAN, HOWARD H. *Effective Communication.* Englewood Cliffs, N.J.: Prentice-Hall, Inc., 1953.

DONNELLY, F. P. *Persuasive Speech.* New York: P. J. Kenedy & Sons, 1931.

GORRELL, ROBERT M., and LAIRD, CHARLTON. *Modern English Handbook.* Englewood Cliffs, N.J.: Prentice-Hall, Inc., 1956.

GRANT, PHILIP S., et al. *Correctness and Precision in Writing.* Boston: Houghton Mifflin Company, 1955.

GRAY, GILES W., and BRADEN, WALDO W. *Public Speaking: Principles and Practice.* New York: Harper & Brothers, 1951.

HART, JOHN S. *A Manual of Composition and Rhetoric.* Philadelphia: Eldredge and Brother, 1871.

HILL, ADAMS S. *The Principles of Rhetoric and Their Application.* New York: Harper & Brothers, 1879.

HODGES, JOHN C. *Harbrace College Handbook.* New York: Harcourt, Brace & Co., 1946.

JENSEN, DANA O., *et al. Modern Composition and Rhetoric.* Boston: Houghton Mifflin Company, 1933.

JOHNSON, ROY I., *et al. Communication: Handling Ideas Effectively.* New York: McGraw-Hill Book Company, Inc., 1956.

KALLSEN, THEODORE J. *Modern Rhetoric and Usage.* New York: Henry Holt & Co., Inc., 1955.

LEGGETT, GLENN, *et al. Prentice-Hall Handbook for Writers.* 2nd ed. Englewood Cliffs, N.J.: Prentice-Hall, Inc., 1954.

MARTIN, JOHN. *Business and Professional Speaking.* New York: Harper & Brothers, 1956.

McBURNEY, JAMES H., and HANCE, KENNETH G. *Discussion in Human Affairs.* New York: Harper & Brothers, 1950.

MURPHY, KARL M. *Modern Business Letters.* Boston: Houghton Mifflin Company, 1956.

PENCE, RAYMOND W. *College Composition.* New York: The Macmillan Company, 1930.

RANKIN, THOMAS E., *et al. College Composition.* New York: Harper & Brothers, 1929.

SARRETT, LEW, and FOSTER, WILLIAM T. *Basic Principles of Speech.* 2nd ed., rev. Boston: Houghton Mifflin Company, 1946.

SATTLER, WILLIAM M., and MILLER, N. EDD. *Discussion and Conference.* Englewood Cliffs, N.J.: Prentice-Hall, Inc., 1954.

SHAABER, M. A. *The Art of Writing Business Letters.* Boston: Houghton Mifflin Company, 1931.

SHERMAN, THEODORE A. *Modern Technical Writing.* Englewood Cliffs, N.J.: Prentice-Hall, Inc., 1955.

TAFT, KENDALL B., *et al., The Techniques of Communication.* New York: Rinehart & Company, Inc., 1946.

THOMAS, JOSEPH M., *et al. Composition for College Students.* 4th ed., rev. New York: The Macmillan Company, 1937.

THOMPSON, A. R. *Handbook of Public Speaking.* 2nd ed., rev. New York: Harper & Brothers, 1949.

THOMPSON, WAYNE N. *Fundamentals of Communication.* New York: McGraw-Hill Book Company, Inc., 1957.

WAGNER, RUSSEL H., and ARNOLD, CARROLL C. *Handbook of Group Discussion.* Boston: Houghton Mifflin Company, 1950.

Bibliography

WEAVER, RICHARD M. *Composition: A Course in Writing and Rhetoric.* New York: Henry Holt & Co., Inc., 1957.

WESTLY, BRUCE. *News Editing.* Boston: Houghton Mifflin Company, 1953.

WOODS, GEORGE B. *A College Handbook of Writing.* New York: Doubleday & Company, Inc., 1922.

————, and TURNER, ARTHUR. *The Odyssey Handbook and Guide to Writing.* New York: The Odyssey Press, Inc., 1956.